My Pants Are Wet, But
I Didn't Do It!

My Pants Are Wet, But
I Didn't Do It!

by
George Wilkins

Illustrations by Wendy

Bright Mountain Books, Inc.
Asheville, North Carolina

Portions of this book have appeared previously as George Wilkins' column
in *The Times-News* of Hendersonville, North Carolina

To my Wendys, my Dinky, and their friends . . .

"I am not interested in controlling children; I am only interested in
them controlling themselves."

The World of Children

Come with me when your heart is blue;
Lose the worries that really don't matter.
When you can't imagine what to do,
Lose them in a childish chatter.

Would you believe this place I've found
To take my soul—this place that heals
When the worldly cares would bear me down—
Where noise sounds and laughter peals?

It pulls me back to a scene forgotten—
A place where small children play.
It is my refuge—my secret garden—
Where all small children stay.

Contents

What This Is All About

"The Cardinal is a bright red bird who eats harmful insects. The Cardinal builds nests. He is usually appointed by the Pope. Popes are usually bishops and arch-bishops."

The above statement is an eight-year-old girl's definition of a red bird. She knew what she wanted—she just didn't know when to stop!

Small children will say almost anything, and they always believe it is true. After discovering this I adopted the attitude of never being surprised by anything I saw or heard from them during the many years I spent as principal of Bruce Drysdale Elementary School in Hendersonville, North Carolina.

One day a six year old came into my office very distressed. He stated very solemnly, "My pants are wet, but I didn't do it!" Then a parent sent in an excuse that read, "Johnny was sick because he was absent." However, best of all was the note from Betty: "Dere Prisabel, I lov you!"

These three small incidents caused me to start keeping

notes about all the extraordinary happenings at school. I first shared many of these gems in a book I published in 1980 under the title *Dere Prisabel (or) My Pants Are Wet, But I Didn't Do It!* Since it has now been out of print for several years, I wanted to reprint it for those who missed it the first time around.

People are so worried about why Johnny can or cannot read that this source of humor escapes them. Perhaps the thoughts that follow—scattered carelessly by adults and innocently by children—may wash away some cobwebs of adult blindness, either by a tear of sentiment or a flood of honest laughter.

So this book is made up of excuses and sayings from and about school children as to why they were or were not late or absent and why they did or didn't do what they were supposed to do. I've also included several slightly altered newspaper columns which I wrote for the Hendersonville *Times-News* which express some of my philosophies about education.

Small children repeat what they think they have heard and strive diligently to please their elders. The results can be very funny, extremely touching, or even painfully poignant.

Can you picture the first grader who wants desperately to learn to read the first day of school so the next can be spent doing something new? And the beginner who starts to tire of school and tells his mother he will like school tomorrow, because "we don't go tomorrow."

Children have peculiar ways of making excuses. When she couldn't read all of her words, Susie explained the words wouldn't come out right because the dentist had pulled a tooth, messing up her "wide-enough muscles."

2

And this excuse is typical: "My Joe was kept home because of illness, either his own or that imagined by his father."

When a first-grade girl slid down the big climbing rope too fast, she shouted, "Oh! That hurt my underwear!"

Hear what Share Time brought out one day: "I woke up last night and heard a strange snoring noise. I went into mama's room, and there was our good friend and neighbor, John, spending the night with her!"

P.E. becomes tiresome to small children very quickly. They can express it very well: "Can I stop doing pushups? My nose is tired!"

Their conversations offer endless eye-openers:

First grader: "Look at those Guinea pigs kissing, and they're both girls."
Another: "They're just friends. It doesn't matter."
First: "You sure don't know anything about life!"

When you ask where they live, you will be told in all seriousness, "You go to that corner, past the store with the sign, turn there, go where the mean dog growls, turn up the hill where Joe hurt himself that day, a little more, and there's my house. And my phone number is 265438-79522."

After you finish reading this book, you will start to know what school is all about. And take it from me, it's not all readin', 'ritin', and 'rithmetic!

If It Rains, Stay Home!

If it rains while you're home for lunch, there will be no school this afternoon.

When I went to school, this rule really did apply! I went home for lunch every day. If it rained during lunch, you did not go back for the afternoon. If it rained before lunch, I would sneak out and run home so I wouldn't have to go to school that afternoon.

There was only one kid worse off than I was when I was in the first grade. He was the type who got to school first every morning and was the last to go home. He smelled bad and his nose was always running. There was something in his blood that kept him from getting sick. You know the type—never missed a day of school. His teachers hated him. I'll never forget the teacher telling him, "Sit down, shut up, and don't even think unless I tell you to do so."

There was a little girl, Thelma, who lived just down the street from me when we were growing up. She whipped me about every day because she was bigger than I was. Later when she taught for me, I never thought to get even.

I never did learn to write very well. My hand never

could stay with my head or something. I can give you an example of how badly I write—even my doctor can't read my writing!

***

When I started teaching, I felt there were many truths I had to give to my students. Since my first assignment was those impressionable eighth graders, I had fertile ground. Whatever I told them would be the gospel! Or so I thought they believed.

Sandy was the star athlete on all our teams. When he entered a contest, everything went our way. He was one of those naturals that happens to a school once in a long while. Our basketball team had not lost a game and the last, biggest game of the year was today. All we had to do was win this last game.

In my classroom there was a very strict rule—don't ever climb out the window or you would suffer the consequences. Guess who went out the window? Guess who got caught? And guess who, without thinking, said, "You don't get to play today"?

We sat there after school, crying together, while the cheers from the gym reached our ears. We could tell the cheers weren't for our team. The ending was predictable—we lost. Without Sandy, we had no chance.

It was truly heartbreaking! We got up to go and I put my hand on his shoulder. "Sandy, I'm certain you have learned a real lesson today. What is it?"

He looked me straight in the eye and said very solemnly, "When I get big enough, I'm gonna beat the crap outta you for making me miss that ball game!"

***

My second year of teaching eighth grade was another experience of learning how little I knew about teaching. I had prepared an excellent lesson for science. It was an achievement of which I was justly proud. The students sat there quietly for about ten minutes. Then Carl, one of my troublemakers, got out of his seat and started pacing around the room. I demanded, "Carl, what do you think you're doing?"

He replied, "You're boring the devil out of me."

When I entered the room one morning, there were Carl and Buddy, toe to toe, fighting furiously. I grabbed them and escorted them to the office. When I returned to the room, the students were killing themselves laughing. I asked them, "What is so funny? Fighting is no laughing matter!"

One of them said, "When you walked into the room and saw them fighting, you said, 'What the h— is going on in here?'"

***

But time has helped me, especially after they got me out of the classroom and into being a principal. I got a letter from one class not long ago. It went this way: "Dear Mr. Wilkins—You are the goodest principal we ever had. We hope you will be better next year!"

I have reached that stage where forgetting things has become a habit. This isn't very helpful at school when trusting mothers expect you to deliver messages that somehow never get delivered. Sarah told me she lost her memory and had "ambrosia." Another told me the same thing, only she had "Ebeneezer."

Children really are so sophisticated these days—not

smarter, just more knowledgeable. Bill was standing where Bill was not supposed to be standing after school. I told him he couldn't stand there and wait, to go over and stand with the other children. He retorted, "My mother picks me up here. This is where I'm supposed to wait."

I then said, "Well, you can't stand here and wait. Go over where the other children are!"

His next remark put me in my place. "The principal told me I could wait here!"

Dere Prisabel

There are many satisfactions in school work that make the burdens bearable. Sometimes it is just a little smile from a five year old or maybe a note from a grateful mother. Maybe it's from a first grader who has finally learned to read and write: "Dere Mr. Wilkins, I like you for my Prisabel!" Or from the second grader who told me, "What I don't like about school is going home!"

The principal occupies an enviable position in that he is regarded as a king, a lord, the owner and holder of all that lunch money. If you do something for a child and the cards fall right, you are seen as supernatural for helping that particular child. But, some of the thanks are honest and very welcome. The following note is from a grateful mother who does really like us and our school:

> The principal is usually the forgotten man or the man to blame. In this case, let him be the man to thank. Thank you for running such a fine school. The teachers are superb and dedicated, a reflection of your

leadership. The atmosphere of the entire school is 'have fun while you learn.' That is so important with the children in the early grades. But, perhaps the best compliment is the one they pay you when they say you understand them and care about them. And they love you for it.

Those are the letters you never throw away. I still have this one from a third-grade girl:

you are a very nice cute man. you are not maen like the other principal. I wish you were my father. you are a pussycat do you no that pussycat, love, Eva.

But, there are the other kinds too—ones you do not want or like to get, and there is nothing you can do when you get them because they are not signed:

Dear Principal, Just a reminder that the next time my daughter has to stand out in the cold waiting for me to pick her up some hell is going to take place on that hill. You no good set of half-educated fools don't have no business in a school building. Don't see why the blacks don't complain about your segregated hiring of black teachers. They are just as highly educated as most of your kind. Haven't hired one since you called yourself integrated. Don't start telling a bunch of lies when hell breaks loose in this little Jim Crow town controlled by a bunch of diehard southern hyprocrits I hope they burn it with all you no good sinners fastened up on the inside.

What really hurts is that schools exist for the purpose of eliminating ignorance.

***

Many notes seem to expect the impossible. We are always asked not to let their child do this or that because it's not good for them, or they'll get hurt, or it'll itch unless the medicine goes on at exactly 10:30. Such as:

Don't let Jamie fall on her buttocks because her backbone protrudes out.

Dere pnincple, please don't let Carl pick his nose. It has been bleeding.

Bill couldn't wear no shoes. It still isn't well so see he doesn't run as much as you can.

Dear Principal, Will you please take care of Tim for me? He can't take any lick on the head or play hard.

Please make Jeff do his work. Spank him and make him listen. He knows his colors at home. That's why I'm sending him, to learn, not to play.

***

Two boys were begging me not to punish them. The first pleaded, "Please don't whip us this time!"

Then the second one chimed in with, "And don't whip us next time, either!"

***

A valentine note: "Mr. Wilkins, you are the best principal I ever had!" (Incidentally, the only one too!)

***

"I'd like to be the principal 'cause he can whistle anywhere and anytime he wants!"

***

Laurel told me, "I like you even if you are a turkey."

***

"Why are the flags up everywhere today?"
"'Cause it's the principal's birthday!"

***

The teacher had just asked who was famous with a birthday in October. The first answer was "God!"

When the teacher said no, another child remarked, "I know someone more important than that!"

When the teacher asked who that would be, he replied, "The principal!"

***

Robert, a very small first grader, came into the office sobbing his heart out. His older brother had forgotten and left him after school. He was all alone! He lived so far away! What should he do? He was told to sit down; surely his big brother would be back for him very soon.

Sure enough, after a very few minutes, James came into the office looking for Robert. Robert was overjoyed and threw his arms around James! No more tears now! James took his younger brother's hand and off they went, Robert chattering and grinning. His "big" brother had come back for him. The odd part was—James was three inches shorter than Robert!

***

One mother was really mad with me. She told me her son had been in first grade for three months without a desk and now would have a curved backbone for the rest of his life.

***

After a five year old showed me a magic trick, he stated, "Now, I'm going to show this to your principal," and proceeded into the secretary's office!

***

One of the best presents I received for my birthday was from Julie—a live frog wrapped in beautiful paper all ready to jump as soon as the paper was removed.

***

I spoke to a third-grade class about the natives in the South Pacific during World War II. A girl wrote to express her thanks:

> Dear Mr. Wilkins, Thank you very much for talking with us. I imagine you had a very nice time when you were younger. You probably enjoyed the hula girls the most.

***

Carolyn, the secretary, has a sign on her door that reads "General Office." A seven year old rushed in and demanded, "I want to see the General!"

***

I had to spend a month in a wheelchair going all over the school for my daily tasks. The first day I ventured forth without it, one little fellow wanted to know, "Where's your wheelbarrow?"

***

A third grader wrote a letter to me: "We love you so much we wanted to give you a hundred dollars, but we did not have the money!" (It's nice to be loved!)

***

Most children are threatened by their parents with terrible actions by that monster, the principal, before they ever come to school. Many times I have been asked by the new children where my "spanking machine" is. Once I completely explained it to two new boys—I did not have one, that would not be right, children did not need that kind of punishment, etc. It was an excellent job of telling that I did not and could not have a machine such as they described. When I paused for breath, one immediately asked, "Yeah, but where do you keep it?"

***

Ronnie would not say his name. I finally asked him what his mother called him. He brightened up and replied, "Wonnie." Then he practiced his phonics for speech class. He rolled out his R's. "RRR, RRR, RRR- Wabbit! I'm getting my R's weal good!"

***

Carolyn, the secretary, had to go somewhere so I was left with all of the responsibilities of the office for a while. Soon I discovered how involved this was. A seven-year-old girl had broken one of her dress straps. Finally I got out the needle and thread and happily sewed away until it was fixed. She said a thank you and skipped out.

***

One of my lawyer friends kept getting his daughter to school later and later each day. I wrote him a note which said:

Dear Lunday's Daddy, Please make Lunday come to school a little earlier. The teacher is going to skin both our heads.

At the bottom of my note came back the reply:

Dear Lunday's Principal, Clear—concise—tactful. Pointed, but painless. A masterful composition. But, you should have sealed and addressed the envelope, because now I've been skinned at home, too!

***

Another friend whose grandchildren came to our school wrote me a tongue-in-cheek exercise in phonics:

Der gorg—i no sum folks fin fault with r skuls. i fur 1 think they r tops. Now u tak mi grandsun, tarry, that's dock's kid, ben goin to skul 2 weks and kan reed that first book. of korse he kums frum gud redin stock. i wud like 2 tak him fishin for 2 weks an giv him a vakation an let the other kids katch up. What du u think about this as i wont to du the rite thing. Luv, earl, senior.

**

One small child with an earache was told to go over to the radiator to warm her ear. When the teacher came for her, she exclaimed, "The principal let me put my ear on their generator."

**

This note to the principal is one of my favorites. It was not really asking for an excused absence, but was rather just an explanation:

Neither Kathy nor Jamie have an acceptable excuse for being out of school yesterday. Since playing hooky has never been legal, always gotten a person into a heap of trouble and has always been a lot of fun we don't have any excuse. Except that yesterday seemed to be the logical day to play hooky. Days like yesterday people have to make their own sunshine. Please excuse us. Everybody should be allowed to play hooky at least once in their life. This was Kathy and Jamie's first time, my second. I'll have to say it's still a lot of fun to play hooky!

Kathy, Jamie and Granny

**

Fran, who lived about two miles away on the other side of town, came to me and said, "You know my four-year-old brother, Bill, likes to ride my bicycle."

I told her that was nice.

She then said, "Yes, and he's outside on it right now! Would you call my mother?"

**

Two days after the Christmas holidays, I received a note for which I had no answer: "My boy told me you had given him a whipping because he did not bring a toy to Share Time."

**

On the outside of a homemade birthday card was a cheerful, but scraggly, "Happy Birthday!" I opened it to find the message, "I hope you can read what I wrote on the front."

**

I always greeted each child as we met in the hallway. Today, Jeff didn't care for my greeting. I said, "Hello, Sir!"

He stopped, glared at me, and replied, "My name is Jeff!"

**

I told Lolita my dog was brown and white. She then told me, "I have two dogs, six cats, and two turtles. Their colors are black, white, gray, black and white, gray, black and white, gray and black green."

**

A third-grade boy told me a kindergarten girl was his uncle. I asked, "Do you mean your aunt?"

He stuttered, "No! Uh . . . Yes, I mean she's . . . I'm her uncle."

I Wuz Sic

This book started with an absentee note which read, "Johnny was sick because he was absent." Just a small error, but when you see twenty or more a day, some are bound to be classics.

"Mary was running a temperature and became a little horse." Of course, a word or two would explain everything—or would it? Over the years I have found that usually a word or two to explain only thoroughly confuses it more. "She was out because she wasn't feeling too bad. I mean, she still ain't feeling too good."

First, the simple ones: "Carolyn sic—she stay home," "Mary ben sick," and "Robert was sike," and "Fir I sick." Then there are the more complex ones: "Rusty had the flew Feb. 9, 10, 11 and 12th and was absent both days."

***

"She had flue of stunk and bile movement too."

***

"Terry was not in school 'cause she was sick at her stump."

★★★

"Annie cut her toe thirday and couldn't come on Firday." (I think she cut her tongue!)

★★★

New kind of medicine: "Dear teacher, Sonya is still not well so I want her to have her meditation immediately after lunch."

★★★

"Sharonsorethroughhead hurt."

★★★

"Mary has the diatthea. She is some better but still go a lot to the bathroom. I come see you as soon as I feel better."

★★★

"It was raining too hard for Susie to come to school. Besides she couldn't find no shoe."

★★★

"Richard had the cold flue. Please keep him warm this week."

★★★

"I was out with athlete's foot."
"Why?"
"'Cause I run so fast!"

★★★

The teachers all liked this note: "Please excuse Lucy. She had side pussy [pleurisy!]."

★★★

"May had a fever, sore throat, head ache and upset stomach. Her brother was also sick, fever and sore throat. Her sister had a low-grade fever and ached all over. I wasn't feeling the best either, sore throat and fever. There must be the flue going around . . . her father even got hot last night."

* * *

"I was absent because I had the pain!"

* * *

"We had to keep Beth home yesterday to nip a cold before it got started. She may still infect the whole class—ha!"

* * *

"Allen was out of school because his clothes were dirty. I ave to wash by hand the baby wasn't old enough to do so."

* * *

"Robert was out with a bug yesterday. I thought it best to keep him home with it." (I'll bet they played all day!)

* * *

"Ronald was quite sick. He had a touch of bronchitis, sinus trouble, a cold and a sore throat. He was running a high fever, his lips were parched broken out with fever blisters and he had to stay in bed."

* * *

Sam wrote his own excuse. The truant officer told him that was forgery. Sam retorted, "No, sir, it's not! I signed my own name to it!"

* * *

18

"Barbar ha a up stet stome and vome had a feaver she voice of stome hope you can read this."

And the next day: "Barba had fear and her kidney are bad."

***

"Rebcca out and cain't drink milk It make her stump soar and hert so let her drink tea."

***

"Please excuse Jimmy for being. It's his father's fault."

***

"Please excuse Blanche from P.E. She fell out of a tree and misplaced her hip."

***

"Sylvia was in bed sick with her head and stomach. Will send her tomorrow if she keeps improvising."

***

"My son should not take P.E. today. Please execute him."

***

"Dear school, pleas ackus John for being absent on Jan. 28, 29, 30, 32 and 33."

***

"Sandra's absence was due to teeth. So in the future her presents may be interrupted."

***

"I was absent yesterday because mama was cooking beans and didn't finish."

***

"Edie was out because she had a toothache and I didn't get any rest at all."

***

"Marva has been sick and has been under the doctor." (For years I had heard this one, but never got written proof until Marva.)

***

"Minnie was out because I was sick."

***

"Please excuse Freddie. He was out with his tonsils." (Probably a double date!)

***

"Please excuse Joe from being sick. His ear and head were hurting him because his neck was broken. So see that no one hits him above the belt." Believe it or not, later in the year someone did tackle this boy while playing and his neck healed!

***

"Rhonda was fine this weekend but got to vomiting this morning before coming to school. If she gets too sick to stay at school, call her a taxi if you know one that's cheap."

***

"Please excuse Cindy for yesterday. We slept late, had a flat tire, the electricity was off, no heat and it was snowing."

***

"Please don't let no one hit Barbara on the head the doctor said."

***

After Halloween came the note from the dentist about his daughter, "Too much treating and not enough tricks! Julie had to have a tooth removed. Down with candy! Let's have more tricks!"

***

"Please excuse Linda as it was necessary."

***

"Patsy is getting symphony of the flu."

***

"The reson Barbara was out Thursday and Friday is because her daddy's brother died and we buried her on Sunday."

***

"Chris had an acre in his side."

***

Would you believe this one? "Reason I was sick—300 degree fever." And . . .

Carolyn, the secretary, told me Jon's temperature was 102.3 or something like that. When I asked Jon what she had said, he told me, "I believe she said it was 176 degrees." And . . .

Wayne said he didn't come to school yesterday because his temperature was 146 degrees.

***

One child told me she had "ammonia."

***

"Please excuse Joe for being absent. He fell at work and hurt it bad!"

***

"Onna didn't come to school last week 'cause as soon as I got my relief check we went on vacation."

***

For only the second time in thirty years: "Ellen is not to take P.E. today for she is still under the doctor."

***

"Dear teacher, I am sending Johnny today. If you start getting sick, call me."

***

"Jennie has a cough, so give it to her when she coughs."

***

"Will you please watch and see if Jimmy's bowels move?"

***

Ossie was concerned: "I've got pink eye; does that mean I'll go to hell?"

I Wuz Late

For some obscure reason, tardiness is considered to be a cardinal sin in schools, or so children and their parents soon come to believe. So naturally tardiness creates a rash of unbelievable and senseless excuses.

"Stephen's tardiness is due to X-rays."

And from the usually late child came a new one: "Mama got lost bringing me this morning."

***

"David and Karen are late because David pitched a real bad fit! He didn't want to come."

***

Joe had a remark to make about another child being late: "Golly, Sandra's retarded again!"

***

"The reason I was late is because I got up too early."

***

"Please excuse Bill for not wearing shoes. This made him late and it's still not too well. See that no one steps on his toe meaning to."

***

23

Angie was fifteen minutes late. "Please excuse us for Angie's tardiness. We hope she didn't get too far behind in her work."

***

There is nothing parents could say that would surprise us. "Melissa was late because she had a stomach ack; but I think it was mostly gas."

***

One little fellow was wise to write his own excuse this way: "Mrs. Miller, You is a nice teacher to the hole world!"

***

What I believe to be the best excuse we ever got was one turned in by a child who knew she had to bring one. However, because she could not read, she simply picked up a note at home her father had written to an older sister, and handed it to her teacher as her tardy excuse. It read:

Dearest daughter, I hope this is your happiest birthday ever! Just because you're sixteen! We love you very much and want you to have many more happy days. The presents we gave you are easy to give to you—telling you we love you is very hard to say sometimes, so we wrote it!

The tardy excuse was accepted (and returned).

***

"I'm late because I had a doctor's apartment."

***

"Please excuse Joe 'cause he oversleep and he had to walk to school and I had a tantrum for him."

24

I Hate Parents!

Everyone has always laughed when I told them, "I hate parents!" Then they snicker when I say, "I hate teachers, also!" But that's another story about teachers. Why people laugh is beyond my comprehension. They must think I'm kidding.

I'm a parent. I have five children and twelve grandchildren. So I really must be fooling. But listen . . .

Children have as their closest friends, protectors, and advisers their parents. These parents come in all shapes, sizes, and colors. However, there is one thing they all have in common: There is nothing they will believe bad about their child when he starts to school if they haven't discovered it earlier. If you are not a parent or can't believe this, just ask one of them. There is a strange carry-over effect about this knowledge throughout their entire school career. It has its greatest effect during the first two or three years.

Parents have several ways to hide this problem. They move their child to another school. They move their child to another room. They talk around it as if it did not exist. "My child is not getting what he needs at your school," or "his teacher doesn't understand him." Trouble is, sometimes they are right.

Parents are apt to disbelieve anything, all and everything bad or different about their child in school. Later in his school career, he finally does something to prove what was told them earlier—something their little baby would never do!

The child usually is not the problem in this sort of situation. It's just his upbringing and there is one way to prevent most of it—communicate! Teachers and parents will say things about each other that never should have been said and wouldn't ever be said if a pattern of conferences was arranged early. The child learns quickly to take both sides of the fence. We had a child who wrote this story:

"My mother says crickets will eat your clothes. My teacher says crickets will not eat your clothes. I believe both of them."

A parent will do well to question, listen, believe, or at least think about what the teacher tells her about her child. Better yet, the teacher and parent should sit down and discuss Junior at the first sign of trouble. Until we have this sit-down-and-talk-it-out, we will operate our schools in an atmosphere of "he's going to be a devil, troublemaker, delinquent, etc." Most of us tend to fly off the handle at the least objectionable thing said about our child. That's understandable.

Time seems to prove what teachers say about different

children. If it is only a temporary personality conflict, things will be better next year. However, if the child has the same problems every year, something is wrong. That's when there should he a good get-together to talk things out. And it will not help if father stays away and only mother comes.

Parents should come to a conference with one main thing to learn—how's Junior doing in the classroom. If testing is indicated or parents need to accompany their child to a testing center, then both should agree and both should go.

The federal government in one of its well-intended edicts has forced a system of labeling upon children. The label may never change, especially if it's a bad label, and then your child is stuck with it. It used to be that a child was dumb or just didn't study. Now he's "deprived" or "undermotivated." Let's face it, someone has to do the hard things and someone else is going to have it easier.

One bad example of labeling is the state requirements for labeling a child as "gifted and talented." This wide range of pseudo-rating would allow 35 to 40 percent of the school population into "gifted and talented." It should include only 5 percent. Separation of superior children at an early age is detrimental to a democratic society and should not be encouraged. But it will be done as long as parents believe their child is in the select 5 percent. Superior children should be exploited by no one, especially their parents. I have seen only about seven truly gifted children in my thirty-one years in education. It's a very strange fact that they turned out just the way they themselves wanted to turn out. Most of them merely tolerated their parents.

Parents can avoid this trap of labeling by never telling the teacher how wonderfully smart their precious darling is. "My baby is already reading, so what will you teach him?" We'll try to teach him to be a child—something he probably missed by mother forcing him to read!

Many children learn to read for different reasons. Many do it by themselves. Fine! Each one is uniquely different and does things at different rates and ages. Some are so different they do attract labels that are not so very nice.

The reasons I hate parents go beyond these reasons. The biggest reason I hate parents is because they won't let their children grow. So, let me list a few things parents can do so their children may grow.

Let him walk down the hall by himself. Let him find the car by himself. Let him learn responsibility for himself, the sooner the better. Practice responsibility before he comes to school. If he loses a dollar that was for lunch that's OK. We'll feed him. He is supposed to make mistakes.

Let him do the talking when he is asked a question. Don't talk down about the school in front of him. Don't say bad things about the teacher when he is around to hear. Letting him be present when he is the center of controversy is very damaging to his self-respect.

Don't break the school rules. They were made to protect your child. Bringing and picking up on time is also a matter of protection and safety for your child. In a few short years the schools will be in the day-care business. However, now our subjects are academic, not babysitting.

Parents are not always to blame. There are far too

many teachers who do not put children first (I also hate teachers!). Even principals do stupid things once in awhile!

The poem that follows seems to fit the situation.

Children Are—So Different

Their faces are the same year after year,
Yet, each face is so different!
They do the same things year after year,
Yet, each thing is so different!

They say the same things year after year,
Yet, each word is so different!
Yes, there are answers for all their problems,
Yet, each problem is so different!

How could I ever forget any of them?
Yet, I do, and they are each so different!
I have loved all of them the same
Yet, each is loved, oh, so differently!

The years began to fly by, all the same,
Yet, each minute is so different!
The parents are all the same year after year,
Yes, they really are!

I Hate Teachers!

Someone asked me a few days ago why I hated teachers. It is something I hadn't thought about in a long time, for my theme song was "I hate parents!" However, hating teachers is what got me into education in the first place. "If only I could ever be a principal, I'd get even and show all those old maids what was what!"

My teachers were all old maids and were ugly and shapeless! I don't believe I knew what shape meant. But this fact also has colored my approach in hiring new teachers. Since most teachers are women, there is the built-in factor of "who-can-deal-with-people-who-are-women?" Don't get me wrong. I love women. In fact there is a rule in my hiring folio that states, "A teacher, to be hired, must be smart or good-looking," Now you can understand why I had the best looking faculty in the state!

But to get back to how my first school years affected my ideas of school and what teachers should do for children:

First of all I was the youngest of nine raised during the Depression. You can imagine what I got to eat and wear—drumsticks and hand-me-downs. I loved drumsticks, but I had six sisters!

You must understand I had a poor self-concept and was very backward at five. My mother sent me to school a year earlier than the legal age. How she did that will never be understood! So you can see what happened when I stepped into a new world where ridicule, anger, shouting, name calling, and other such self-esteem builders were routine every day.

My entire first-grade adventure was with the end of my nose in a small chalked circle on the blackboard. After about ten minutes my breath would condense on the board and run down into a nice little puddle on the chalk tray! I'd get a spanking for being so nasty! Then back to the ol' nose job. In another few minutes the old bat would grab me and scream, "Why are you making those faces? Are you trying to be funny?" I was just trying to keep from breathing!

In the second grade I learned all about bathrooms and going—how to and how not to! You raised one or two fingers. I raised three one day. She didn't let me go all day. That year we were all bad. We were so bad one day she wouldn't let any of us go. A chain reaction started and before the janitor could finish mopping, she was crying. Everyone was afraid but me—I laughed out loud I was so glad! I got a beating for being the ringleader.

A couple years later I had a real fire breather! A mean ol' bird with fangs, talons, and spikes on her shoes to stomp kids with. She reminded me of the original Chicago Bears—the entire defensive line! I stayed in place that year!

My music teacher was a very small lady who rapped your head. She demanded you learn all those little black notes, but you didn't dare sing! "What do you mean by dancing? Sit still and listen!"

I had one teacher who thought dirt was a curse word. A poor student who was also dirty never stood a chance in her room. Of course we were all dirty and smelly. She would clean our fingernails with a very sharp railroad spike!

She sent a note home with a below-the-tracks student that said to "please clean Johnny up for he smelled so bad the class was suffering." That mother wrote back to Miss Clean, "Don't worry about the way my Johnny smells. He smells just like his daddy. That's the trouble with you old maid school teachers. You don't know what a real he-man smells like!"

I finally arrived in high school with a violent distrust of anything that stood in front of a classroom. However, when I went to my first class, freshman English, there she stood—Miss America! They had imported a real movie star to be my teacher! She didn't like me, but I never realized that. I got lousy grades, but who cared as long as I could sit there and stare at her!

Then she married the dumb coach and my world ended! He was the one who couldn't even spell his own name. We counted the "uh's" he said in class one day. In forty minutes he said *uh* two hundred and seventeen times! For the first two weeks I thought I was in a speech correction class!

If you got caught smoking in the bathroom, it was a sure whipping. In fact, if the principal saw you uptown with a pack in your pocket, he'd take them away from you, and you'd get a beating the next day at school. (I'm certain he sold them!) Today some schools have smoking areas and the kids still get caught in the bathrooms, not for using the pot, but for smoking it!

The way I feel about educating children was definitely affected by my early school experiences. I have tried to keep children from having these same trials. Don't misinterpret my words or intentions. Children have to behave and be decent. They must be cultured and have manners. But they must also have teachers who know that kids are people too.

Most teachers do not fit into these frightening categories. However, most all do on different days and different occasions. All I have done here is to say why I hate teachers. Principals fit in here somewhere.

Teachers are not supposed to be human or to have human emotions. If they were, the legislators and the public would pay them what they deserve, and we would have classrooms in which we could teach children as it should be!

But then, I also hate politicians!

The Truth and Other Lies

What small children tell you is the truth when they say it word by word. Sometimes the only error may be the arrangement of the words. Take the first grader who came into the office and asked, "Has a big eraser with a pencil on it been turned in?" Or—"My sister kicked me in the stomach. Ever since then I've had bad breath." Or—"My mother can't join the PTA 'cause she has the flu."

***

When the class had finished collecting flowers and insects, one child exclaimed, "Look! I caught three Praying Mothers!"

***

The younger they are, the more naive, more open, and funnier. One kindergartner looked at the just-baked cupcakes, some of which had fallen, and said very sadly, "Some of 'em died."

***

The difference between a cow and a bull: "One of them gives milk and the other butter."

***

Some of them are sly and worldly wise. The music teacher was going through all the Valentine songs, and after a long practice session asked the class which song they would like to sing. David quickly spouted out, "Silent Night!"

* * *

The test contained the question "Who was Christopher Columbus?" The best answer was: "Oh, he was in my kindergarten class last year. Sat right next to me!"

* * *

She brought an orchid that her grandfather gave her for Valentine's Day. The teacher remarked how nice it was and asked if her grandfather had a greenhouse. She answered, "No, ma'am, it's white with a green roof."

* * *

Joey said his doctor told him he had ulcers and wasn't to have anymore gin and tonics with his grandfather.

* * *

Five-year-old Janice's new dress was very low-cut in back. She told us it was almost down to her breasts!

* * *

A first grader took home a paper with a "D" on it. Mother asked, "What are you doing with that on your paper?"
Answer: "I didn't do it—the teacher put it there!"

* * *

"I'm glad we're taking home our books! Now I can prove to my mother I can read."

* * *

"Did you know my great-uncle was 995 years old?"
"No, what was his name?"
"Methuselah!"

***

"My mother's in the hospital with pneumonia."
"That's nothing! My daddy's in the pen for writing bad checks!"

***

Wayne was asked if he knew who Roy Rogers was. Ken butted in and shouted, "Roy Rogers? I know him. My grandmother dates him!"

***

Reid told Carolyn, "My mother's older than you!"
"How do you know that, Reid?" The secretary knew that Reid's mother actually was younger than she.
"'Cause she's got more wrinkles than you—she's got 'em all over her body!"

***

"Teacher, did you know my dog's gonna have ten kittens?"

***

Two boys walking home after the Halloween party: "Now I know why Joe gave me this pumpkin. It's retarded!"

***

"What do you want for your eighth birthday, Susie?"
"A Barbie doll and a catcher's mitt."
"Why a catcher's mitt?"
"Because I don't have one!"

***

"I have to get a lunch ticket today."

"Why?"

"'Cause my daddy took my lunch box by mistake!"

***

She was trying to get Tyrone to understand two from two was zero. She said, "If you had two apples, and you gave me two apples, how many apples would you have left?"

Tyrone answered, "Two!"

So finally the teacher reached down on the ground, picked up two rocks, handed them to him, and said, "Here, Tyrone, are two apples. Now give me two apples, Tyrone."

Tyrone reached down, picked up two more rocks and handed them to her!

***

"If you want to know how flabby your brain is, feel your leg muscles!"

***

Keith saw no one to help him, so he spread the very large American flag out on the ground, folded it over very carefully, brushed it off at each fold to get the trash off and then triangled it very neatly. Then he brought it in to me. I asked him where he learned to fold a flag so well. He told me, "I did the very best I know how!" I sent him on his way with a perfect score!

***

At 2:00: "I have to be home before 4:00 or my mother will beat me. So, I'm leaving right now!"

Teacher: "No, you're not! Sit down!"

***

One day after school the secretary was looking for two boys. A first-grade boy waiting for his ride exclaimed, "I saw 'em! I saw 'em!"

So hand in hand they walked to the end of the hallway. He mused, "Well, they were here."

She asked, "When?"

"Yesterday about 3:00."

***

"What rhymes with bat?"

"I don't know."

"Like [hand gestures] big woman!"

"Oh! Pregnant!"

***

Emily got a good report card: "Teacher, you sure are a sweet grader!"

***

One of our teachers has the name Christopher. One of her students asked her if Christopher Columbus was her daddy.

***

Teacher (at lunch): "We certainly forgot our manners today!"

Albert: "I forgot my straw!"

***

Bert enjoyed his lunch. "For lunch we had cornbread. Then we had cornbread with strawberries on it!"

***

"Boy, she sure runs a tight ship!"

"Yeah, and it ain't the Good Ship Lollipop either!"

***

The class had thoroughly discussed the Dewey Decimal System and where the books were in the library. The librarian quizzed them. "John, if you come through the door and look immediately to the left on the second shelf, what do you find?"

John's reply: "Books!"

* * *

It was the first day of school, and I was calling out the names of the new first graders, one by one. One little fellow told me he hadn't heard his name yet. I told him to sit right in the front row as his name would come up soon. He waited another minute and interrupted me saying, "You'd better hurry, 'cause I have to go to the bathroom real bad!"

* * *

"What'd you do in kindergarten?"
"Got ready for first grade and learned to be quiet."
"What happened to those who weren't quiet?"
"They flunked kindergarten!"

* * *

Roger told Kathy, his girl friend, he had named his new puppy after her. She told the teacher she had never been so embarrassed before!

* * *

"My grandmother is real, real old!"
"How old is she?"
"Fifty-two!"

* * *

Q: "Why do we have Thanksgiving?"
A: "Because George Washington died on his birthday."

* * *

"For Share Time today I want to tell about the nice trip me and my mama went on with her boy friend. We went camping to a log cabin in the woods and I got the top bunk all to myself!"

* * *

"I eat boogers at home, but not at school."

* * *

Bill wanted to sit at the P.E. instructor's desk while the movie was being shown. The teacher noticed Bill was slowly and carefully slipping a marker pen out of the desk and into his pocket. When the film was over, the teacher went over to Bill and told him the pen was there a minute ago and was now gone. Bill thought a second and said, "Louis took it!"

Louis came over and declared, "Bill is a liar and a thief!"

Then the teacher "accidentally" bumped into Bill and felt his pocket. "Bill, here's my pen in your pocket. How did it get there?"

Bill's reply: "Well, I really put it in my pocket to keep Louis from stealing it."

* * *

The startled teacher watched Steven pull a hundred dollar bill from his pocket. "My father wanted me to bring this to Share Time."

* * *

A kindergartner rushed over to the teacher and exclaimed, "Scratch right there, quick!"

* * *

"My little brother came with me to get a rabies shot."

* * *

40

A small jar of alcohol was broken in the room. After three or four sniffs, Kim said, "That smells like the stuff daddy drinks all the time."

Not to be outdone Mary spoke up. "The policemans had to help my daddy get to work one night when he went to sleep from drinking too much of that stuff."

***

Q: "Why do you wear a belt wrapped around you three times?"

A: "To hold up my pants!"

***

Our janitor, Jim, was rather large in the stomach. Two girls were discussing his hat which he wore most of the time.

Cindy: "Jim's hair is growing."

Jan: "It's 'cause he not wearing his ol' hat. He shouldn't have worn it last year—his hair would be a lot longer."

Cindy: "Yeah, and besides that, I think he's gonna have a baby!"

***

"Can I go to the sharpener? My pencil's numb."

***

It was terribly cold that morning. Stephanie came into the office with blue hands. She was told to go warm them over our radiator. After a few minutes I looked and there she was, rubbing her hands together over the typewriter.

***

Q: "How do you show bravery?"

A: "By going to school more!"

***

It was American Education Week. We were to have a large group of professional men as our guests. Four fancy cars drove into our parking circle about 10:00. About fifteen well-dressed men walked up the sidewalk just outside our kindergarten rooms. Henry, very excited, shouted, "Golly, look at all the used-car salesmen!"

***

Greg's shoe sole was loose and flapping. He said, "Looka here! The hem's clean outta my shoe."

***

He was so happy in kindergarten until he found out they would soon be taking naps. "I knew there was a catch to it somewhere!"

***

Martin brought a lightning bug to school in a jar. When they went out on the playground, Greg found two more. Without Martin knowing it, Greg placed them in the jar. Then Martin looked into the jar and exclaimed, "Lordy, my lightning bug done laid two babies!"

***

"Guess what? My neighbor is getting pregnant next Saturday!"

***

After explaining an assignment in the new math thoroughly, teacher told the students to take their books home for "homework." The next day they were eagerly telling all about doing their new math. That is, all but James who said, "My mama didn't know anything about this new math and said for me to do my homework at school from now on."

***

I made an announcement on the P.A. system to all the rooms. The last sentence was garbled. When the teacher asked what I had said, Kevin answered, "Man, I dunno, but he sure chewed it up!"

***

"For Halloween my mother is going to dress up like a reindeer and my father like an idiot."

***

They were smelling liquids and guessing what they could be, then tasting. Tom: "Good God! That's water!"

***

Our high school's woman P.E. teacher worked in our summer program one year. She learned very quickly about very small children. Four third-grade boys were swinging too high, which was against her rules. As a punishment they were told to do ten pushups. Some of the other boys noticed them straining and groaning. They immediately asked the teacher if they could also do pushups. Soon the ground was alive with boys doing pushups. The ones being punished then asked if they could do ten more.

***

One six year old: "Do you have a girl friend yet?" Another: "No, but I'm getting into it!"

***

"Bernard, what are you going to dress up like for Halloween?"
"A debil."
"Oh, you're not a devil, are you?"
"My mama says I is!"

***

"I brushed my teeth three times this morning when I got up."

"Why?"

"The P.E. teacher said to brush 'em three times a day!"

* * *

The story was about the secret Jack had in his box. Soon the class would know what was in the box if they read more of the story.

"Why don't we know what's in the box?"

Of course Bernard answered, "'Cause we ain't turned the page yet!"

* * *

The arithmetic paper was all wrong. Teacher: "Did you get any help?"

Tony: "Yes'm, my uncle."

"Did he say anything?"

"Yes'm. He said, 'Every damn one of 'em's wrong!'"

* * *

"My mother works at the bank."

"No kidding. Which branch?"

"She don't work at no branch. She works at the bank."

* * *

Our preacher came to eat with his five year old. As they went through the lunch line, young Greg noticed something back in the kitchen. "What the hell is that?"

The startled manager asked him to repeat what he had said. So Greg obliged: "What the hell is that?"

His father very meekly said, "His mother taught him that."

* * *

44

John: "Bull's gonna pick me up today."
Teacher: "Who is Bull?"
John: "Just Bull. You know, he shouldn't be called Bull. He's a man, not a horse!"

***

Q: "Tell me something about George Washington.
A: "He discovered America."
Another five year old: "Hah, hah! Naw, he didn't. Abe Lincoln did that."

***

"Dear Susan, I love you lovely. You are so sweet. You are pritty. You make me look like a frog. I hope you will marry me!"

***

"Teacher, we went to a Saint Patrick's Day birthday party for my mother and everything was colored green, even the cake! Guess what color my 'you-know-what' was the next day?"
Her friend then topped it off by asking, "Teacher, what's a 'you-know-what'?"

***

A kindergartner whose leg was hurt: "My leg jumped off the roof."

***

"Yes, I did spit on Brian. But I told him he could spit on me!"

***

Viewing a very pregnant guinea pig:
Q: "What are those things?"
A: "Those are milk bottles."

***

He was counting. The teacher finally told him to skip over the thirties. So he started skipping around the room counting, "Thirty-one, thirty-two . . ."

She said, "No! I mean jump over to the forties."

So he did: "Thirty-one, [jump], thirty-two, [jump], thirty-three . . ."

***

"What would you do with a dirty wife?"

"Throw her in the garbage!"

***

A father came late to get his son after school. He had looked all around the school when I saw him. I told him maybe his son had gone back into the classroom. He started to go inside the school, took three steps, stopped, and muttered, "Damn it! He's home sick today!"

***

"I'd like to have a conference with you, Teacher."

"Why?"

"To find out how I'm doing!"

***

Jennifer was being kind to her brother after she had won an Easter coloring contest: "My brother might have won a prize too, if he hadn't colored Jesus's hair green!"

***

"My mother is a nurse."

"Does she run a nursery?"

***

A new first-grade club: "See The Girls' Butts Club."

***

Roger: "That band concert made my Christmas birth-day the very best yet!"

"When is your birthday?"

"May 15th!"

***

Gina said there were some funny words written in the concrete tunnel. The teacher investigated and told her that was "French." The next day Gina rushed to the teacher and reported, "David's writing French in the tunnel again!"

***

A first-grade boy who was very proud of his father explained, "My father is the biggest man in the world! He is 8' 10" tall. . or is it 10' 8" . . . or . . .?"

***

Mike rushed into the office and demanded, "I need a lunch ticket quick!" Then to himself he muttered, "Mama told me to keep part of this dollar bill for milk money." He then tore the dollar bill in half and offered the other half to Carolyn, a very astonished secretary!

***

Q: "When does the 4th of July come?"

A: "Oh, about the 10th of June."

***

Two second graders came to the playground very late from their special reading class. One had a steaming hot cup of coffee and the other, a giant milk shake. When asked for an explanation, the answer was offered very quickly, "We went our secret way!" They had crossed two highways and three very busy corners to a nearby sand-wich shop!

***

He stuttered and lisped, but was he having fun. He rushed up to his teacher and declared, "Me got on me horse, me shot and me robbed the bank!"

"No, Horace. *I* got on *my* horse and *I* shot and *I* robbed the bank."

"No, you ain't done it. You ain't got no horse and no gun!"

***

The class was discussing traffic jams. Kenny said it was terrible at 5:00. The teacher wanted to know why it was so bad then. He answered, "That's when the mamas are taking all the maids home!"

***

The music teacher was explaining how composers often told stories by their music. Joe said sadly, "I wish they wouldn't!"

***

A third-grade boy who loved the Green Bay Packers sent a "mad" letter to the ABC TV network complaining that he didn't get to see his favorite on TV anymore. He signed the letter "Unknown!" Then he sealed it up and proceeded to put his full name and return address on the envelope. In about ten days he received a very nice letter from the ABC front office. The salutation began, "Dear UNKNOWN."

***

Her father was in the hospital. "He's gonna die April 8th."

When asked to explain, she replied, "well, he said he'd never reach his fortieth birthday and that's on April 9th!"

***

48

"My daddy went to Washington, and I told him to tell the President not to have those silly press conferences on TV so I could see my shows."

* * *

The story was about a child who had been asleep for two years.
Sally: "Was she in a coma?"
John: "Nope, she was in a bed!"

* * *

"I want to show this money my daddy got for fighting in the war." (A Confederate bill!)

* * *

Timmy was always a car, a plane, anything but a Timmy. He was walking down the hall backwards, hands clasped together, moving them back and forth, making a swishing noise. When asked, he said, "I'm a windshield wiper!"

* * *

When John was told certain religious denominations do not celebrate birthdays, he wanted to know, "What are they, Russians or something?"

* * *

"Elmo, why have you and Bobby been beating on Kimberly? She's just a little girl."
"Yeah, but she stepped on my favorite kind of bug!"

* * *

When cautioned to brush his teeth, this helpful child stated, "because if you don't, you'll get diarrhea."

* * *

This one was from a seven year old who wanted something for Share Time: "My aunt got married. Now she's not horsing around anymore!"

***

An educational truth: "It doesn't hurt me if I pinch you!"

***

When the hostages were released from Iran, Amanda remarked, "The ostriches were flown out of Iran today!"

***

When Susie lost a baby tooth, she was very emphatic about what she would do. "I'm gonna put it under my pillow so the Tooth Fag will leave me some money!"

***

Millicent told her mother she was studying very hard. "Mama, I've been constipating very hard on my school work."

***

William had already been in two fights one day. The teacher tried to warn the P.E. instructor, but before she could get the words out, he was fighting again. This time he picked on Teksha, a girl. She whipped him soundly. No one interfered. Everyone was happy except William.

The Picture Man

How does the "picture man" take so many good pictures? All those wiggly, squirmy children would drive the sanest man crazy after just a few minutes! At our school we had a natural-born clown who took our pictures for years.

The secretary listed everything he said. He rambled on and on without repeating himself long after she got tired of writing. Each child got a different treatment:

Is your wife jealous?

See you left your teeth at home.

The draft board wants this picture.

Did you shave this morning?

Pull that ol' massive chest back!

I want a starry-eyed smile!

Have you had a neck operation? Oh! That's a turtle-neck!

You're not mad at me, are you?

Okay, Cotton-top, hit that seat!

Look at me, Bright Eyes!

Who licked the red off your candy?

You're gonna have to stop batting your eyelashes; you're hitting my hair!

If freckles were pennies, you'd be in good shape.

Have you been playing with matches? I see a singed place in your hair.

I see you left your partial at home.

Don't want to see the top of your head—your wife may see you have dandruff.

Are you a flower child? I see a daisy in your hair.

Say "women."

There you go, ol' smacky mouth!

You carry your weight well—well out in front!

Button your love buttons. They're your "wife-catchers."

Have you got a false tooth in your pocket?

Have you been married long?

Are you the little girl all those boys have been chasing all morning?

You had your eyes closed! Your husband will think all you do is sleep!

You're flat-headed right there. You have a "kiss curl."

Put all three hands in your lap!

What are you doing with lipstick on your collar?

You look like the last rose of summer that was frost-bit last night.

Sit down, Heavy—you look like you've been standing beside the bean plate. Don't you bite me!

You got your head on sideways this morning!

That's *dun-lapped*—done lapped over your belt.

Is your husband doing okay?

Best-looking thing I've seen all morning—haven't opened my eyes yet.

What kind of cigarettes do you smoke?

Did you shave last night?

Send your wife over here next.

Hair looks real pretty—a lot like my German shepherd.

Your cigarettes are showing in your top pocket.

Now smile like a mule eating briars!

You look a lot better since you got married.

Say "I'm sweet—please—peanuts—boys—worms—sissy-britches—Aloysius Brown!"

He called each child by a different name. Boys might be called Curly-Bill, Chester, Big Hoss, Little Max, Nehru, Gabby, Bomar, Goober, Flash, Arnold, Cat-Man, Ralph, Fred, Alfred the Great, Gomer, Virgil, Lloyd, George, Jethro, Sweety, and Wild. The girls were Molly, Juanita, Agnes, Myrtle, Sugar-Burger, Freida, Maudie, Ella-Mae, Alfreeda, Wanda, Jessica, Blondie, Norma Jean, Missie, Martha Ann, Sally, and Rose. It was not so much that these names were so uncommon, but rather the way he drawled them out and pronounced them very slowly and distinctly that kept the smiles coming.

Just for excitement he would call some of the bigger boys by girls' names: Agnes, Missie, Maudie, Myrtle, etc. which got a lot of guffaws and giggles. It certainly didn't help discipline much, but the smiles on the pictures were real. He would ask teachers to give him that Friday-afternoon smile or to smile like the day-after-payday. He was a real character and made life worth while that day!

This was certainly part of the school scene—a very important and educational segment. We were most fortunate to have a man who loved his job and children also. It is a shame all of us can't deal with children this way.

Leese Is What It Is

Donald came into my office and told me that he and every member of his family had "leese"!

When you go into a school and see most of the staff vigorously, but tentatively, scratching their heads, you can bet your life lice have arrived. Everyone is afraid they are next. The dreaded "galloping dandruff" disease has arrived!

When the students' hats come to school without the students, you know something is wrong. Or you see their hair waving with no breeze, it's not hair tonic! We all joke about it, laugh, and make fun. However, we are secretly horrified by the thought that those little grayish things could be parading around on our heads.

One nice lady, after eating lunch with her daughter at school, brushed a table companion's hair because it was unruly—such a pretty little girl needed her hair to look nice. Then the mother put the brush back into her pocketbook. Not too many days later guess who inherited what that tangled hair must have had? Everybody says it's no sin to get 'em, only to keep 'em! How absolutely true. There's no way to prevent lice if you don't know they're around. Then all of a sudden, there are several cases.

Sometimes the advice you get about how to get rid of them is not strong enough. The medicine label may not be easy to understand or may seem a little vague. Believe me, you must follow all directions, keep looking, and seven or eight days after washing, do so again—and keep looking.

I must reassure parents: schools do not give out, furnish, or sell lice in any form. Parents are inclined to blame schools for lice. Believe me, I hate them as badly as parents do, and we're not going to give them out if we can help it! We don't like this problem for children, and we certainly don't give it to them. (I would like to give it to a few parents sometimes.)

We always call the health department when lice are found, and every child gets a thorough going over. The health nurse comes running and scratches her head all day. We do too. She inspects every contact and all siblings and their contacts.

There was one mother who indicated she had to restrain herself from coming to me because her child got lice. Her inference being she was saving me trouble. Her child had them twice in four weeks—not too uncommon, especially when the treatment is not complete or the contact is still around.

Marge told me everyone in her family had lice except her father. In fact, they had each had lice twice, and he didn't get them. I thought something was peculiar until he came one day to pick her up. He was the original Kojak—a real polished baldy!

John told us he had 'em all over him, even in his shoes. Sam wanted to know how high they could jump.

One kindergarten child told at Share Time that at his sister's wedding everyone threw lice all over the bride and groom.

One kindergartner told how he and his buddy looked for them in each other's hair. He didn't have any so his buddy gave him some of his!

A mother collected them in a butter tub to see how long they would live. When her child looked into the tub, she proudly exclaimed, "Oh, boy! What a collection!"

After many daily inspections, this little girl would shy away from her mother every time she came near. "Oh, no! Not again!"

Where the little creatures started or how they continue on and on is a mystery. I believe they vacation just like we do. When it turns cold and everyone is close together, they sneak out and start pestering everyone again.

Contrary to common belief, lice do not bark like dogs or sting like bees, and carrying a "Roach Motel" will not help. A good medicine shampoo (another in seven or eight days) and a thorough washing of everything in your house is what is needed. The little buggers can hang around for quite a few hours and reinfect, so don't forget the second shampoo. They do make your head itch terribly! If you don't want to check Johnny's head, wait until he scratches continuously, then shampoo.

So, when you notice birds landing on and pecking away at your child's head, get out the old reading glass and see what you can find. Then you too can say, "Leese is what it is!"

Religion and Christmas

Religion and schools are not supposed to mix or have anything to do with each other. However, there is no way to keep them apart in the public schools, especially with our country's history and godly culture.

I have had teachers who on Monday morning would teach Sunday school lessons to all those who missed it on Sunday, and I could almost guarantee that a majority of our classes had some religious daily beginning. Regardless of the edicts, God manages to slip in when you least expect him.

One of the first notes I ever received from a child was a large drawing of a cross under which was written, "Jesus died for you and me!"

We once took our entire student body to a "Blessing of the Animals" at the church next door. Most of our children had never seen anything so impressive. When the procession of robed and hatted priests came into view around the corner of the church, one little first-grade girl shouted, "Oh, Lordy! Here comes God!" Then another screamed, "And Jesus is right behind him!"

***

When she got home, Susie asked her mother if she had prayed for her (she was extremely hyperactive):

Mother: "Yes, Susie, I prayed very hard for you."

Susie: "Well, it didn't do any good. I was in trouble all day!"

***

A six year old kept talking about suicide this and suicide that. Finally her sister asked why she was so interested in suicide. She replied, "Why not? Wasn't he one of the disciples?"

***

Our P.E. teacher was monitoring three students who were waiting for their rides after school. Just across the street, six children from our local Roman Catholic school were on their way home dressed in their dark plaid uniforms. As our children stared at them, one asked, "Who are they?"

Another answered, "Those are Christian children!"

The teacher quickly asked, "Aren't you a Christian?"

He, just as quickly, replied, "Heck no! I'm a Baptist!"

***

A mother reported this conversation to me. Her son was saying his prayers and included a part about his poor grades at school. When she cautioned him to pray harder, he asked, "Why? Ain't the Lord's fault! It's the teacher!"

***

They bowed their heads to say a prayer for lunch. The aide peeked as usual to see who was misbehaving. There was D.J., standing, head erect, hand over heart, very solemnly repeating the Pledge of Allegiance.

***

A prayer, overheard, from a boy who was waiting for his punishment: "I thanked about what I done and I thanked I done wrong!"

***

This boy had been promised a spanking which he never received after he handed me this prayer: "Oh, Lord, please spare my soul and make Mr. Wilkins change his mind!"

***

Priscilla, always a cut-up when the teacher was out of the room, lost no time in running around the room when her teacher was summoned to the telephone. I punched in the P.A. system to that room and asked, "Prissy, are you in your seat?" No answer, but there was a scurrying sound. So, a little louder, "Prissy, are you in your seat?" Still no answer, so I spoke very loudly and very clearly, "PRISCILLA, ARE YOU IN YOUR SEAT?" This time Prissy replied, very meekly, "Yes, Jesus!"

***

The teacher was trying to force the word *staff*. She used the Bible by saying, "From the Bible comes, 'Thy rod and Thy ___?'"
One little fellow cautiously offered, "Reel?"

***

Everyone was supposed to write stories about billy goats. So Joe wrote, "There were three great men—Shadrack, Meshack, and a Billy goat!"

***

Did you know that "Thanksgiving is when Jesus was born"?

***

Question to the librarian: "Do you have that story about that guy that got hanged on that cross?"

***

I have seen many letters to God, and I have also read that book, so I have included two here as typical of the many we see each year:

> Dear God, Let me spend the night with you tonight and sleep at your house. Mama has been so-o-o ugly to me!

> Dear God, I hope you are filling good. I'm filling good. I'm going to help you God! Love, Greg

***

Story: "I met a fairy one time who gave me a wish. I wished for all the money in the world. I would not give it to anyone but God!"

***

On the bulletin board just outside the office were two silhouettes—George Washington and Abraham Lincoln facing each other. One morning I heard a loud discussion between two second graders:

First: "That's God!"
Second: "No, it's not!"
First: "Yes, it is!"
Second: "I know it isn't, 'cause I know who it really is!"
First: "Who?"
Second: "It's Jesus!"

***

Praying: ". . . and please help my teacher. Mama says with me there, my teacher needs all the help she can get!"

***

Where this came from none of us could understand: "All God does all day long is float around on a cloud, drink wine, and eat deer meat!"

***

Bible reading: ". . . and they were full of despair!"
"Now, what does that mean?" asked the teacher.
Student: "Got a flat tire?"

***

John: "Jesus is Hercules!"
Joe: "No, Hercules is Jesus!"
John: "No! Hercules is Jesus's son!"

***

Joe: "Can Jesus fly?"
Teacher: "Certainly, He can do anything He wants."
Joe: "When I get to Heaven, do you reckon He'll teach me how?"

***

"Teacher, are there bushes in Heaven?"
"Certainly!"
"Do they have switches?"
"Of course!"
"Uh, oh!"

***

"'When I was a child, I spoke as a child.' Now I'm growing up, I'm supposed to act like a grown-up. Heck, I don't wanna grow up!"

***

"What is the Holy Spirit?"
"Only the Shadow knows!"

***

Our P.E. teacher, Jim, always said, "If I say it, it's the truth!" One day in the office he told us, "If I'm not telling the truth, so help me, may lightning strike me!" Everyone immediately backed up (his record wasn't the best). Sure enough, lightning struck a tree outside, shook the building, and caused the phone to ring. Someone shouted, "Don't answer it, Jim, it's God!"

***

Christmas is the most special time of the year for our children. Teachers don't usually try to destroy the fairy story parts of it; moreover, they probably build them up. Children don't forget the real reasons behind Christmas:

> Christmas is the time to think about Jesus and God and good friends but be glad when you get something too. I love Christmas!

> Jesus was born in a manger. That's how Christmas was made!

***

Here is proof positive that spelling is not important. "C is for candoll, R is for rith, I is for icecickels, S is for star, T is for toys, M is for merry! Which all spell Crismas!"

***

Tommy, talking about a little kindergarten Santa: "Man, that's the skinniest Santa I ever seed!"

***

Kindergartner's remarks about his gift to his teacher, "My gift to you smells so good and delicious, you will want to go home and take a bath."

***

"I watched Santa Claus when he sneaked in and got in bed with Mama!"

***

Overheard on the playground: "What'd you tell Santa Claus you wanted for Christmas?"

"A wing."

"A wing? Why a wing?"

"No, a wing for your finger!"

The questioner then turned to the teacher and explained, "She can't say *wing*!"

***

A first grader was writing a letter to Santa. His buddy seated next to him couldn't seem to get any ideas about what to ask Santa, so he decided to copy his friend's paper. The original letter was this: Dear Santa, Please send me a "Johnny Express."

His buddy's copy was like this: Dear Santa, Please send me a "Johnny."!

***

We have many children who, because of their parents' religion, cannot participate in any of our holiday activities or parties or any celebration. We have always tried to observe their desires very carefully, but, as you can imagine, we still manage to overstep the boundaries sometimes. We try not to say or do anything to let the children know how we feel, but it does seem extremely cruel and thoughtless to do this to little children.

One Valentine's Day the teacher forgot and let Jody receive many valentines. She apologized and told Jody she was sorry. Jody answered, "Oh, that's okay, I can get 'em, I just can't give 'em!"

Dear Teacher

There is nothing that has not been asked a teacher. "Dear Teacher, Please send me a receipt for all my child's lunch money for this past year. I need it for income tax purposes."

Or: "Please loan me $2.00 till next week."

Almost all these notes began "Dear Teacher." Almost never do they reveal any knowledge of the teacher's real name. But the teachers generally lump all parents into a "Dear Parent" category, so everything comes out even.

***

"Aubrey has a nail in her foot. Don't let her jump around and play on it."

***

"Don't let Wayne go out and play. He has a bad head cold in his throat."

***

"Last night someone fired a shotgun into our house. The police feel the children would be better off at school. But please keep Mary in at recess."

***

"Please see Bobby through another lunch today. His daddy has been down with his kidneys all week and has broke us."

***

Of course teachers don't always understand the correct things to do either. Note to the office: "Charleen is upchucking every few minutes. Should she go home?"

Or: "Joan was out yesterday because she was stuck with a pencil. Do you think she'll have lead poisoning?"

***

The teacher finally had to wash Joe and then put clean clothes on him. He had needed this for a long time. He forgot to take his dirty things home with him that afternoon. The next day teacher got this note from mother: "Send me Joe's things you took off him or there will be trouble, and don't take anything off him again. P.S. I don't want to haft to send after the law!"

***

"Dear Coach, I learned a great lesson today from your speech. I'm now going the join the YMCA this year. I hope I never knew that you didn't know that we can use so many things for the use of that."

***

"If you don't whip that boy for hitting Alan on the arm, I going to do something about it!"

***

We got this little note every Monday for three years without ever getting a dime: "Please charge Sally's lunches this week and I will pay Friday."

***

Sometimes parents reach out very strongly to teachers for help with their children. The following letter is quite touching in its appeal for help:

Dear teacher, I no you will not understand this I cannot read very much. I had a hard time in school and I did not learn anything in school. So would you help Teresa. Please. I try to help her all I can and I want to help but I can't because I don't no much so I can't. Please.

***

"Please excuse David today at 1:00 as he is sick."

***

This little girl expressed her sorrow because of a snow day. "Dear Teacher, I am writing because of snow today. This morning John came running in my room and woke me up. He panted and said Margie its snowing. I woke up and started to cry because I love school and I love you!"

***

After reading a note from Marilyn's father, the teacher said, "Your father writes beautifully!"
"I know, that's why mama married him!"

***

Roxanne told her teacher she was allergic to P.E. and had a note to prove it from her father. It stated, "I am sick, dad."

***

Being adopted was a pleasant experience for this child: "Dear teacher May I bring some cookies for the class this coming Friday? It's my adopted birthday!"

***

This mother knew what was what. "I took Billy to the doctor an the doctor fill the papers an he found nothing wrong. Billy does dip snuff once in a while, but I'm sure he's not the only one. I know Billy doesn't do to well in school but that's the best he can do. What he needs is more help from you."

***

"Pat was okay over the weekend. She didn't have a fever and felt good. Her red cheeks was finally diagnosed as too much grandfather's beard!"

***

From a seven year old: "I love Mike very much and I would be much happier if I could sit by him could I?
"P.S. Me and Mike are going to get married. We planned to do it in kindergarten so if I do not get to sit by him, he won't marry me."

***

Evidently this man told his wife to quit meddling in the school's affairs. He wrote the teacher this letter:

Dear Ms. Jones: My wife visited with you recently. She inquired why homework assignments had been discontinued in your class, and it seemed some other parents objected to this practice. I would like to urge you to disregard what parents say and to teach your class according to your own concepts and good training.

***

"My little boy lost his gloves yesterday. I want you to go to all the teachers and organize a search for them."

***

"Dear Mrs. Smith, You are a sweet teacher. You are not nice, you are just a plain sweet teacher!"

***

Our school was named for a fine local man, Bruce Drysdale, who was head of our school board and was instrumental in obtaining monies for many school projects. He would come to our school and go into the classrooms. The children would crawl all over him and they both loved it! When he died, many children wrote about him. This third grader slipped in a mention of him in an end-of-year letter to his teacher:

> Dear Teacher: Thank you for teaching us this year, but I'm glad I'll be going because I have spent three years in this school but I liked it while it lasted. One day when I'm going to college I will remember you. Mr. Drysdale, rest his soul, put a lot into this school, but when he died, Mr. Wilkins took over and put it together again!

***

"Mrs. Johnson, You're going to think I've flipped. But my husband is interested in buying a Corvette. There is one at school in the teachers' parking lot. Could you find out what year it is? It's very pretty. He wants one with a body style like that one!"

***

"Teacher, please get mad as a wet hen. I want to see what one looks like."

***

We still have not figured this one out: "Will you please give Irvin every day?"

***

A note on our Swish and Spit program: "Jean has my permission to squish and split."

***

"Where is James this afternoon?" the teacher asked the class.

Susie explained, "Oh, he had to go home after P.E. He got sick from chewing tobacco."

***

If you don't believe teachers know all about their students, listen to this tale.

The class had been swimming at the Y. It was time to leave. After everyone had their clothes on, we had one pair of extremely dirty underpants left over. I picked them up very carefully with two fingers and carried them out into the vestibule where their teacher was waiting. "Mrs. Smith, here's an extra pair of pants."

Mrs. Smith took one look, twirled around, pointed her finger accusingly and said, "Jimmy! Go put your underpants on immediately!"

***

One teacher who had retired liked to substitute a lot. Kevin came into her class to return a record from his class. When he returned to his own classroom, his teacher asked him, "Did you give the record to Mrs. J.?"

Kevin: "Nope. I gave it to that woman who's always hanging around here!"

***

One teacher complained to the P.E. teacher that he was teaching P.E. all wrong because the children were having fun!

***

We had a lot of trouble teaching Chris to skip. The P.E. teacher spent extra time with him. One day they came to my office to show his skill. I told him to skip everywhere he went because he was doing so well. Off down the hall he skipped to his room. The teacher came into the hallway and asked him,"Just what do you think you're doing?" I doubt he ever skipped again!

Telephone
Troubles

The telephone is a wonderful instrument. It can say things between two people that couldn't possibly be said face to face. It allows school parents to confront the principal and his teachers with unanswerable accusations. From the school's vantage point, we can take down many complex messages which are promptly forgotten and never delivered.

We used to let children use our telephone for almost any reason until finally the tears washed all the numbers off and one child threw up on it.

The most revealing phone call I ever received was from an irate father who demanded, "What I want to know is where in hell did my son learn that damn cuss word he brought home?"

On the other hand, one mother called just after the day had started to tell me Ricky was not absent, but her husband had brought him once, then intercepted him on the way back home walking. He told his father the teacher told him to go back home because his hair was not combed!

***

One mother called and wanted to know, "My five year old told me she had something for dessert that was hard on the outside, watery on the inside, thick like mud and was orange!" The answer was peach cobbler!

***

"My son, Paul, told me Billy Jones bought Paul's toy car for a one-dollar bill. I have the dollar here and it's a fifty-dollar bill!!" I had just received a phone call from Mrs. Jones, frantic because she was missing a fifty-dollar bill!

***

An angel-faced girl slipped into my office just as school was starting. "May I please use the phone?" Why? No answer, but she held up her little foot shyly. Still on her feet were the dainty little rabbit bedroom slippers she had failed to take off!

***

Lou's mother called to explain Lou brought her lunch because we served the same lunch every day in the cafeteria!

***

Mother asked me to tell Johnny's sister not to wait for him for he had come home sick from school. She also let me know, "I had a party last night, and no one got to bed before ten o'clock. That's why Johnny's so sluggish today! Well, I'd better get out the enema syringe. Aren't you glad you're not a little boy anymore?" Believe me, I was glad I was a big boy and didn't live at her house!

***

Mother: "Is Mrs. Smith's room warm today?"

Answer: "Yes, ma'am."

Mother: "Well, I don't want to send Debbie unless it is because she's sick."

Answer: "Please don't send her if she's sick."

Mother: "I have to. She'll fail if I don't!"

***

A third grader was monitoring the phone for us one day. She told us a man called from Washington about somebody's death. She couldn't remember his name, what he wanted, or if he'd call back. She said he didn't talk very plain.

***

While an irate father was telling me about some wrong which had befallen his son, I inadvertently cut off the connection (I had called him). I hurriedly called him again for he had been breathing fire at the time! He just laughed and told me how foolish he felt when the phone buzzed as if I had gotten fed up with his tirade!

***

Teacher called a first grader's home to determine the reason for the child's absence. She inquired, "Is Angie there?"

A little voice answered, "Yes'm, here's me!"

What's in a Name? Everything!

Until we reached five and could go to school, our names were something we accepted without question and without a second thought. Names were something that never really mattered, not of major importance and certainly not requiring much attention or thought. We heard our names and came running.

Then we started school and suddenly discovered what a name was and what it wasn't. Some of us answered to personal nicknames like, "Come here, Stupid!" Then, some of us were called by our middle names. Now you were in for trouble! For some unknown reason, legally first names are what it's all about. But anyway, school has started, and I don't know what my name is, and I can't answer to that strange sound they keep calling me!

Yes, names are what we go by or what people call us, and usually what we don't like to hear, especially after school starts. People have a bad habit of naming their children for people they like or for some ancestor whose name meant money for themselves. Whatever the reason you're stuck with it. When you are young, there's nothing you can do about it. When you're old enough to change it, you are either accustomed to it or don't wish to make a fuss—besides, your friends wouldn't know you if you did change it.

We all have a bad habit of ridiculing or laughing at those individuals whose names are different or unusual. This is devastating to a five year old who is just starting school. There is nothing he can do about it. Whatever name his parents gave to him, that's the name he will carry.

It is not my intention to ridicule or make fun of anyone's name. It's bad enough if a person doesn't like his label without me adding to his misery. But I have been fascinated by names ever since I ran across a little migrant child whose real name was Ten-Cents. So I have collected and filed names to share with everyone. Many of these names are "made-up" names. In school we have been swamped with many strange and different names. "Roots" may have partially caused this. Most children are taught, as they should be, to be proud of their names. There is a proud history and a rich heritage to many of these names. Some, however, are pure fiction—parents', not mine.

Frequency of certain names seems to go in cycles. This year the big thing in names may be Jon or Joanne. Next year it may be Billy or Ron. To be absolutely cool it must be a made-up name. The name doesn't have to be different, but the spelling must be original. For example: you may be Shawn, Schonn, or Sean.

The most popular names for children today seem to be Chris and Christy. It is amazing to me that in the past thirty-one years only one child has gone through our school with the name John Henry and only two named Joe Louis.

Teachers have a corner on Judy and Pat, but their parents have also been original. We have a Bay and a Bizzy. Then we have La Muriel Daena, Omie, Adonica Dale, and V.D. To top it off, we have one nice lady whose real name is Jessie James.

Not long ago a lady came into the office to register her daughter for school. She told me the last name. I wrote it down. "What is her first name?" The answer came, "Julie-Ann, with a hyphen!" (Not too unusual). "And what is her middle name?" The answer: "Kristie Sue."

Another five year old registered one year with a most unusual name. When I asked her mother where it came from, she told me she had made it up. Her name was Celestial Moonrose, but Bathsheba Princess is my all-time favorite!

On my list are: Kunte Kinte Isis Shazam, Bilalian Irashama, Kenyetta Vernee, Latisha Tarra, Laquanna Lalatoya, Schnell, Daya Lamanique, Schronda, Tarji, Prinz Nikia, Venus Shundias, Bree Danelle, Nitiki, TeaRa, Shrondreka, Jamal, Signe, Teffgre Ardul, Rahsaan Duane, Constantina Shamona, Sakaya, Marsarah Oilsa, Mongo Smith, Laterisha Latrelle, Kanika Antoyeni, Orion, Enis Onecka La Shaun, Karleff Mazilateef Yeavee, Xavier Deanlee, Tangia Love, Tajakica Vasblate.

And: Havilah Rebekah, Deshawn Adrace, Shanee Lajovan, Maeleangulia Valicee, Kodi Claude, Shareef Rasool, Kemual Shaveh, Loopie, Radames Caquias, Wendy Autumn.

And last of all: Olufunlayo Bolade Bahyyah Kalejaiye. Try that one on for size. We just called her Funlayo.

We heard of a child called "Fee-Mah-Lee." The mother explained she got it off the little girl's hospital bracelet. It was spelled F-E-M-A-L-E!

One thing bothers me. Where'd I get the name George?

For unbelievers, there are twin sisters Aran'gelo and Yelo'gelo which deciphers to "Orange and Yellow Jello"! Then there's Chewbacco and Misty, Autumn, Kissy, Sequence, Sequoia, and Aimee. Then there's Ebony, Spring, Jaylee, Walkup, Asia, Amber, Tegan, Saturday, Tomorrow, and Ellanny.

I have been called many names that sounded like Wilkins—Wilks, Wilkerson, Williams, etc. To make matters worse, the high school principal's name is Wilson. He is more than ten years younger than I am. After my book was first published, Mr. Wilson was standing outside his office when a bubbly freshman boy rushed up to him and spouted, "Mr. Wilson, I really do like that book your daddy wrote!"

Deff-ee-nich-shuns

There are so many misspelled, misquoted and mis-handled words and meanings it would be impossible to record them all. Many are familiar to us, such as "hopper-grasses" for "grasshoppers." But did you know what you should put on hot dogs to make 'em taste better? "Rubbish!"

"Bruce Drysdale" becomes "Broos Bridal." "Usually" goes to "yousle." This may be due to the increase in their use of word-breakage and phonics. Or more likely, it may be that small children just spell the best they can until they are able to spell correctly.

Here are some of my favorite definitions:

Completed: Simple—it means "Done, done!"

Amen: "You're through and God knows it!"

A bitch: a female bird

Generator: one who narrates the story

An exclamation point: constipation mark

A queen: a lady king

The bowels: a, e, i, o, and u

Garden fertilizer: horse remover

***

"I have to get 'bracelets' on my teeth."

***

"What kind of dog is that?"
"A Dobermanpinchme!"

***

"Vibration is when you put a glass of water in the sun and it disappears."

***

"The plural of sheep is goats."

***

A second grader's definition of a prostitute: A lady with one side of her sewed up and the other ain't!

***

"My dog got hurt so we called the vegetarian."

***

"What is a baby horse called?"
"A cow."

***

Teacher: "Will someone please show me how to migrate? What would you do?"
George: "Well, first I'd have to ask my mother!"

***

"When we went to Jorja to werk, . . ."

***

A dog with a pedigree means:
1 - He doesn't like to be petted.
2 - He has no friends.
3 - He came from another planet.
4 - He has no one to play with.
5 - He doesn't like strangers.

***

"Asthma is something like constipation."

***

"What does your aunt call you?"
"Nephew!"
"What is your mother's brother?"
"Uncle!"
"What do you call an unmarried woman?"
"Unhappy!"

***

She broke her arm and then had to wear a "casket."

***

"I want some of that green ice cream—lime shepherd!"

***

The teacher asked for words showing the short "A" sound. The class responded with "Apple. . . At . . ." Then Sonja said, "Aigg!"

***

Susie brought in her tuition payment and reported, "This is my beautician money."

***

"If your eyes hurt, you should put manureen in 'em."
***

First-grader Johnny was explaining a model of the human torso: "This is the large contestants and this is the small."
***

"Teacher, can we play God's ball today?"
***

A broken pencil was explained as "My pencil tore!"
***

"What does adore mean?"
"Teacher, dere's one over dere where's we came in!"
***

The United Parcel man was asked numerous times if he really did bring the chocolate milk (especially the black fellow)!
***

His parent was his "soul" support!
***

Niagara Falls became "Nigger Falls."
***

A first-grade girl watched a boy comb his hair and commented, "I wish I had a crack in my hair!"
***

"I had a shot."
"What kind?"
"A hippopotamus shot!"
***

"David, would you please be a monitor? Jessie, would you be a monitor also?"

"Teacher, can I be a thermometer too?"

***

"Write your "A's" on the paper four times, please." The first paper turned in was like this: "Ass, Ass, Ass, Ass"!

***

The secretary was giving out lunch tickets one morning. To one little fellow it was "Danny" this and "Danny" that and "write Danny on your ticket . . . good-bye, Danny."

Matthew, his brother, said, "His name ain't Danny!"

Of course the secretary was very upset, "What is his name?"

He answered, "Daniel."

***

She kept asking what his father's name was and heard the same answer each time: "Pall Bearer." Then she had to know which funeral parlor and whose funeral. The very patient, exasperated student finally spelled out his father's name: P-A-U-L B-Y-E-R-S!

***

"That's a fire distingquisher!"

***

"What is a widow?"
"A woman whose husband has died."
"Then what is a widower?"
"A woman who has had two husbands die!"

***

Curtis: "These are the times on a clock—1, 2, 3, 4, 5, 6, 7, 8, 9, 10, 11 and 12."

***

Teacher: "What is a mother sheep called?"
Student: "A 'V.'" (Think it over!)

***

"My mother is a prostitute [substitute] teacher!"

***

The class was trying to decide what an outline map of South America looked like. Leon shouted, "It's a po'k chop!"

***

"Did you know our teacher was retiring?"
"No, why?"
"It must mean she's getting old."

***

David's thought for the day: "A dime is ten cents. A nickel is five cents. Money is expensive these days!"

***

"My daddy is half Indian and half human!"

***

On cuss words: "They are hell-thee [healthy] to use."

***

"A hair-a-pist [therapist] is a fellow who tries to help people by talking to them and letting them talk."

A Case of Chicken Snatching

One day or night—no one knows for certain—in a spring not long ago, a small white hen came to Bruce Drysdale to live. It possibly flew or fell off a truckload of chickens passing by on the nearby highway, or possibly came from someone's chicken coop.

Animals running loose at school are not in the best interests of children. We have had gerbils, turtles, and white mice in cages in classrooms. Larger animals such as dogs, cats, and chickens are not usually welcome at school, but whatever or from wherever, we had us a chicken!

We began to get reports of a small white hen pecking away in the school's front yard. At first we put no credence in these "sightings." How could a chicken be at a school by a busy highway in the middle of town? That was just too ridiculous!

But the children insisted that a little white hen was sitting in their pine tree by the kindergarten fence. We

85

had to investigate. Even after I saw it, I couldn't really believe what I had seen. Sure enough, there she was! We had a real live chicken, so we adopted her. (At the same time, I figured after a few days she would disappear.)

For a while it was difficult trying to keep everyone from feeding her at the same time. The songbirds were going crazy—never before had they had so much to eat. The other problem was trying to keep everyone from petting her. Finally we had a schedule worked out—one class kept a pan of water and real chicken feed handy for her, and everyone else could throw out a handful of crumbs occasionally. And there was a no-petting rule, also.

Pretty soon the little white hen could be seen wandering around through groups of children who were playing on the front playground. She would be pecking away trying to find crumbs and worms. I threatened the children with a penalty of death if they chased her!

Occasionally a child would lean down to pet her. She would immediately duck her head, scoot away, wings outstretched, clucking wildly! Then, back to the peck, peck, pecking. We enjoyed this hen—she was funny to watch.

Just beneath the pine where she roosted was a pile of leaves in a briar thicket. One day we noticed she had started a nest. Our chicken was growing up. This was right beside the highway on our front wall. Being so friendly and so close to the highway probably caused her downfall.

After everyone missed seeing her for a few days, I went down to check on her whereabouts. Just outside her nest were a few white feathers scattered about on the ground. Now I suspected the worse!

Some of the kindergarten children told us a "bad boy" had sneaked up and grabbed our chicken and had run off with her "screaming wildly!" Chicken napping—how terrible!

One student who had seen the chicken snatching told me she knew the boy who had stolen her. He lived near her. When I saw him the next day, I told him I was going to swear out a warrant for him unless he brought back our chicken—immediately. It was strictly a "shot in the dark"!

The next day he did bring a chicken back, but not our chicken. It was the smallest, dirtiest, scrawniest chicken I ever saw. When he put it down in our front yard, the poor thing didn't move for ten minutes. Then it tried to limp around looking for a bite to eat. It scratched around for about three days limping and dragging, before it disappeared. We didn't look very long.

We told the children it had gone to chicken heaven where it became a queen. For a long time we talked about our chicken and that bad boy who stole her.

We never forgot our chicken. It didn't have a name. We just called it "Chicken."

Letters, Stories, and Poems

There are many excellent teaching tricks, but one of the best is to have the children write about things they do or make up. The letters, stories, and poems are far superior when they are original.

***

Here are several letters to prominent persons and one not-so-well-known girl:

Dear Gorge Wallas, I saw the man who is called Wallas. He shook my hand and I yelled, yey, Wallas! He gave me a pen and I want your autograph!

Dear President Carter, Down at Rose's store back in the toys there's a Billy Carter Pick-up truck. In the Winn-Dixie there's Billy Carter beer too. We watch you on television.

Dear President Ford, I like your dog. I like you too. I like your dog the best!

Dear President Carter, It is very cold in N.C. I am

hoping to get coal for our heaters soon. Everybody in our family voted for Ford but me. I voted for you. What is it like to be a peanut farmer?

Dear Emilie, Please meet me in Paris when we grow up. We will get married and live together. I will be a cop and a singer. Bring food and water. I will bring a motor cicle and a car. Don't worry I will be all wright to you!

* * *

Some short stories:

Peter was not a good boy. He hid in Mr. McGregor's. Peter eat cabbage!

The funniest thing I ever saw was my dog scratch her behind. The saddest thing I ever saw was my dead dog!

If I were the teacher, I would die because the kids is crazy!

What I like is recess! I like girls! There is something I like about recess and girls!

My cat had five kittens. My next door neighbor had baby kittens too.

* * *

Some longer essays:

Thomas Edison invented many things. He invented the first light bulb. He even invented electricity so that mother could electrick things.

The Eggstink Dinesaour
Long, long ago a dineasaour was caveman's most biggest enname. About a hundred cars did not eggzist. Cavemen did not yuse guns for wepons. They you clubs.

During Easter we went to a farm. I made friends with a yearling and petted four colts. I got to see a new horse and it was a boy and he looked mean but he looked mean because he was breeding four lady horses and he got all mean because one of the lady horses wouldn't let him do it. So he kicked her!

Hummingbird

Once upon a time there was a hummingbird. He always used to humming. One day he had sore throat. His throat turn. That is how a hummingbird got a red throat.

The Oppossum

1 - An opossum is bad tembered.
2 - An Opposum sleeps in hollow trees.
3 - When it heres its enemies, he rolls up into a tite ball.
4 - It has 13 teats and has about 20 babies and if the others don't get to the teats they will suffer!

My mother is very kind to me. She always tucks me in at night. She buys me stuff that I don't need. She uses a belt but sometimes a hickory. I fell in a lake but she pulled me out!

If I were my mother, I would spank my mother and make her wash the dishes. And if I were a snake, I would bite her and she would go to the hospitile and she would haf to get the poison out!

Rain, Rain

Anything will get wet if it is out in the rain. How do I know? My dog tells me so. If my dog had a raincoat, he would not tell me so.

George Washington

George Washington was in the Revolutionary War. When he crossed the Delaware, he was attacked by Indians. And they threw out the Boston tea bags!

Abraham Lincoln

Abraham Lincoln is a good man. When he was a boy, he cut down a cherry tree his father planted. His father did not whip him because he was so honest. When he grew up, he was called honest abe. A very mean man shot him. Three doctors came. They had to lay him sideways he was so huge. It was no use, they could not help it. The next day he died. That was the end of Abraham Lincoln.

***

At a private school near here, one of the sisters told her class the word *frugal* meant "to save." Now they were to write a story using their new word *frugal* in it. One little fellow got up and read his story:

The princess looked out of her prison tower and saw the prince. "Frugal me! Frugal me!" she cried. So he climbed the tower and frugaled her and they lived happily ever after!

***

A third-grade essay:

My Mouth

My mouth is for eating and when it comes to talking it blabbers all the words it knows and seldom ever stops!

***

One of our second-grade teachers made the mistake of getting her class to select their own pictures out of magazines to write stories about. At least, she told me she would never do it that way again. Here is why: Frank cut a large half-page Tampax ad and pasted it at the top of his paper and then proceeded to write his story:

Tampax

One day I had a problem. It was my soap. It was not good enough. I did not like the soap that I had. It was too sweet or too sour. I had to get another soap. Then I found a soap. It was Tampax. It was my dream soap. It was a good soap. I like to use it every day in, day out.

***

Book report on *A Kiss Is Round* by Blossom Budney:

My mother and daddy kiss me goodnight. A ball is round, but why is a kiss round? Because when someone kisses you, your mouth is round!

***

When Mickey Marvin, a pro football player, comes back here to visit his first school, all the children get his autograph and write stories about him. Mickey's first-grade teacher told her class to finish this story: "I Dreamed I Was Mickey Marvin." One girl very painfully wrote this story:

I didn't want to dream I was Mickey Marvin. I wanted to dream I was Wonder Woman. I do not know why I dreamed I was Mickey—I do not want to be a boy! Stop this dream!

***

"If I were a gift, . . ."

If I were a gift, I would be a doll and a little girl would play with me. She would take care of me and

92

she would love me and even though I wasn't alive I would love her too!

If I were a gift, I would be a golf ball! I would give it to my dad. He would play with me a lot. He gets a hole in one all the time because I go in for him! He did it for a living 'cause he was so good with me in his bag!

If I were a gift, I would be a bike. I will give it to my brother so that he would be happy and ride it!

If I were a gift I'd be love. If I were a gift I'd be peace. If I were a gift, I'd stop fights.

The peculiar thing about the above item is that the boy who penned it was one of our worst troublemakers. He was always in hot water about something, usually for fighting or talking back to a teacher. We need some way of getting inside of their minds so we can know to help them when it doesn't seem that's what they want.

***

First-grader Kevin's young grandmother got married again. He was included as part of the ceremony which took place at one of her friend's home. Here is his account of the entire day:

Kevin's Own Story of the Wedding

When I went to Pop Powers house and me and my sister ate our lunch that was candy and pretzels and peanuts. And then it was time for us to go to the wedding. Then we standed and had the wedding. Then me and my sister had cupcakes and punch. Then we talked, then we ate and then we played. Then we watched TV and picked up the weights, then Norman got the rice and one of the girls got some corns. Then we threw it at the car and my dad locked the door. He was the last one to throw the rice. He throws it right when 'Who-Who' got in the car. Then we watched TV and talked. Then we had to go home.

***

Ask a small girl what she believes to be the loveliest thing in the world; then, ask a little boy. Make sure they are about eight years old. One girl's loveliest thing:

> The loveliest thing I know is a rainbow. It grows very low. Its colors are blue, orange, red and pink. It's kinda round. I sometimes think the colors are the rainbow's crown. Its lips are red, and its head is too. Its arms are yellow. It's such a happy little fellow. And when it sinks, I'm sad!

One boy's loveliest thing:

> The loveliest thing I know is my dog. He looks very sad with his bloodshot eyes. He sounds like a drum when I come home because he thumps his tail on the wall. He sounds like a train tooting when he howls!

***

Children write poetry as easily as they do stories if the opportunity is given them frequently enough. I selected these few out of hundreds:

The Bald Man
I bought some Nair to put on my hair,
The next morning I had a great scare.
I bought a toupee, it turning into hay.
My wife had a terrible, terrible day.
She sewed some hair onto my head,
The next morning I was dead!
So why am I talking here today?
I was just faking I was dead yesterday!

Kites fly up, kites fly down,
When you're not flying them, they stay on the ground.
Kites fly high in the air and they don't make a sound.
When I fly my kite, I make it go high,
If the string breaks, oh kite, good-bye!

Spring makes me sing a song
That's not very long.
The thing that makes me sing,
Is spring!

I had a little rabbit, but he ran away one day.
I missed him very much when I went out to play.
One day I went for a walk in the woods.
And there my rabbit stood.
He was under a big pine tree.
I was happy and so was he!

The moon is very far away,
But men may go up there some day.
Nothing grows up there I know,
And there is not even a river to flow.
I always thought there was a man in the moon.
I don't know if that's right, but I may learn soon!

Children will turn in material to a teacher swearing they originated it. I hope the child who wrote this as hers was telling the truth. Sometimes we really don't know.

Me is a good word
It has all the things I have
It does what I do
It thinks what I think
That's why I like me

Fall is here.
The leaves are everywhere.
When we run out to play,
The wind says, "Hey!"
The animals go to their caves,
But we stay out to play!

Eskimos are round and plump
And they have a wobbly rump.
You see them here, you see them there
You oughta see them everywhere.

There was a man.
He had a pan.
He wore it on his head,
But not when he went to bed.
He walked his way
Through night and day.
His name was Johnny Appleseed.
He did a good deed.
He went around to plant his trees,
And he got dirt on his knees!

Symphony

The tuba is a big horn—but it was never born,
All the cymbals—are bigger than thimbles.
A trombone—makes any kind of tone,
A tambourine—is not a machine,
A flute—Makes a high toot,
An oboe—is not a hobo,
A cello—cannot say, "Hello!"
A bassoon—is not round like the moon.
A trumpet—you'd better not bump it,
A gong doesn't go ding-dong,

A violin—isn't a hen
A snare drum—isn't a bum
The little bells—sing fairy tales
A double bass—doesn't have a face,
A french horn—cannot be torn.

***

The class project was to write a poem using one's name. This third-grade girl's name was Tomlinson:

The animal who always stayed out of line
Was the Nosnilmot with the pink behind!
And there his greedy eyes will stare,
They'll look until they get a glare.
So you be careful and you beware
Of the thing that caught the purple hare
The animal who didn't use his mind
The Nosnilmot with the pink behind!

"Happiness Is . . ."

We have had several children die of various causes while going to our school. It is extremely difficult to understand why these little people must leave us so young, and the pain never really goes away. We remember each one, how beautiful they were, and what their short life brought to us.

I remember one girl who was dying of leukemia and was so happy with the parties the class gave her. She said she had such a wonderful time, "It seemed as if a beautiful butterfly had kissed me!" It is sad they must die but wonderful how they all, almost without exception, have accepted what was in store for them.

We have had almost every emotional and mental problem known to man among our students. One seven-year-old girl had set fire to three houses when she came to us. Another had visions and later killed a man when he grew up. We have seen signs of many different sexual deviations even in the kindergartners. These are the exceptions, but they do exist.

Their fathers and mothers drink to excess. They have

no fathers or mothers. Their parents work all the time. One parent was in prison. They live with grandparents. All the odds are against them. The federal government tries to fund programs to help them but then compounds the problem by insisting the people who will teach these underprivileged are their parents.

Children have a built-in courage and resiliency which seems to keep them sane and able to go on to adulthood without succumbing to emotional troubles which would floor most adults. The most calloused and hardhearted man would literally weep at the story of the daily life of some of our students.

The things children are pushed into by selfish parents makes a real-life shocker of a story. But children have a certain quality of survival which seems to carry them through. They may daydream or have other retreats into a fantasy world, but they do not seem to lose their happy slant or hope for more sweetness. We are often exceptionally cruel to our little ones, blundering through mistake after error without realizing the enormity of our guilt.

A child appears to forget these transgressions quickly. At least I hope he forgets. He needs us and wants the warmth of our love no matter how rough it may be. Pity the memory that carries such ideals as selfishness as a prime requisite for adulthood. I pray children don't harbor evil but for a moment, only a fleeting moment.

* * *

A nine-year-old girl whose parents were separated wrote a four-page story about an old cow and two baby calves who stayed with her. You could tell she was writing about her cruel grandmother whom she and her brother stayed with while both parents went their merry way.

* * *

We had a blind child and her classmates expressed her predicament in various ways. One fellow kindergartner wanted to know why she didn't open her eyes. Another quickly explained, "'Cause she's pregnant!"

* * *

Even though she was abused at home, she explained an ugly bump on her arm by "I stayed under the covers last night and didn't get any air."

* * *

"Dear teacher, Jami is not in school because our dog whom we had for ten years died. He took it hard!"

* * *

Eight-year-old girl: "Mama's boy friend wanted me to do things to him, and then he wanted to do things to me. I told mama, but she didn't believe me!"

* * *

Whatever happens at home comes to school. "We'll all have to line up for a whipping when we get home." When asked to explain, he said, "'Cause we all wet the bed last night!"

* * *

"Please excuse John for being absent. His little dog was run over, and he was so distressed. He got little sleep or rest. If he gets too depressed, call me at home."

* * *

"Mama and daddy are not staying together. Daddy would come home but his rent is paid up where he is staying." He continued to give a three-minute description about all their troubles and then broke it off by saying, "Don't ask me about it. It upsets me to talk about it!"

Black and White

When we first integrated, the children spent a lot of time examining each other—touching hair and skin. It was simple curiosity. Mostly we are one big happy family.

***

Some days the elderly black maid picked up Barron. His mother, white, got him the other days. His classmate, Susie, wanted to know why Barron had a black grandmother and a white mother.

***

One of our teachers kept telling stupid Polish jokes in the lounge one day. Our new black teacher finally told her, "Please stop telling those jokes. Don't you know I'm Polish?" The flustered joke teller said, "Oh I'm sorry. I thought you were Jewish!"

***

And of course we tried to overdo it sometimes. Johnny Black, a black child, came into the office and tried to tell the secretary his name. She looked at him and said, "Johnny . . . Brown?"

He said, "Nope, Johnny Black!"

***

After school the usual crowd was waiting for the usual late parents. I noticed a white mother drive up in a huge station wagon, get out, and start for the office in full view of everyone. As usual I stated, "Oh look! Here comes someone's mother." One little black girl said sadly, "Well, that's not my mother 'cause we don't have a station wagon."

***

When we call a mother at work to come get a sick child, we usually ask the child for her mother's name. Once I asked, "What do they call your mother at work?"

The little black girl told me, "They call her 'Nigger'."

Then I stammered, "No, I mean, what is her name?"

She then said, "Sometimes they call her 'Nig' for short!"

***

On her first day of teaching at our school, a black teacher wore some very white panty hose. A mother whose son was in that second-grade room related to me the conversation that afternoon between her son and another boy.

Her son: "I have a colored teacher."

Other boy: "No kidding! What color is she?"

Son: "I dunno—she's white on the bottom and black on the top!"

"I plege elegas..."

This is an essay about patriotism, ignorance, and stupidity. The first is something for which we must be trained. The second is something that can be changed by learning. The third is what I wish we didn't have, for it cannot be changed no matter what you teach or do.

There are many kinds of tea—plain, fancy, spicy, etc. But I had never heard of "Liper Tea." However, I do have more spellings of the same word: *Ledre ty, Lebrty, Libt, Lrete* and *Liber tee*. As you see, it is a word from our Pledge of Allegiance as written by beginning first-grade students.

When children say the Pledge, it is one thing. When they write it, it becomes something entirely different. *Allegiance* becomes *Aelgins, Alegents, Legens, Legs, Alejuns,* or *Ulegens.* The sound is great. The spelling is terrible! So I guess they are learning something.

For a long while I was afraid they were learning nothing or they didn't know what they were saying. With kindergartners, I was right. They didn't. But, by constant repetition and practice, they do learn. They understand well enough to explain. Some learned by first grade and some not until the third. But most know what it's about—why, where, and how we use it.

It disturbs me to see as they get older how they forget

the rules. However, this is an age problem and it passes. It's the adults who really bother me.

When adults show an ignorance about their country's cultural heritage, it's up to us as teachers to retrain them through their children and by example. We show them what is proper, acceptable, and decent. You keep a society viable by obeying its laws, learning its history and mores.

A rather odd fact about humanistic psychology is we all feel a kinship to those who at times show their anger at certain rules—something we'd like to do! At the same time we feel a resentment against them. They are rebelling against things they deem unfair. We resent them because they rebel.

However, when people show a continuing, unreasonable resentment against our cultural mores, we are failing in our teaching. We must grit our teeth, grin, bear it, and try to teach their children better. We can overcome the ignorance. The stupidity we can't touch!

We live in a country where disrespect can be shown to the flag and other national symbols without fear of jail or worse. Where else could this happen? This one fact should turn the disrespect into love. I repeat: this one fact should turn the disrespect into love!

But we deal with stupidity along with ignorance. For this disrespect to be a passing fad is acceptable. For it to continue is inexcusable! For parents to counter-teach it is revolutionary!

Time has passed since many different people showed a flagrant disrespect for all our national symbols. Time has created a vacuum for most of these people, possibly an entire generation. Even now when you go to a parade or an athletic event, people will wear hats, talk, or sit as the flag goes by or the "Star-Spangled Banner" is being played. It's a bigger shame that they set such shining examples. The Olympiad in Los Angeles brought a genuine resurgence of patriotism, but it is fading.

It's time all teachers delivered a little more teaching on how fortunate we are to be living in America. Why don't we prove we aren't in the stupid class?

Lesson on patriotism: People live in communities. They adopt flags and songs to represent their community. They adopt rules for these icons. Succeeding generations change these rules by orderly processes. We call this a democracy.

Lesson Two: We stand for our flag and song. We uncover our heads, be respectful and quiet. This is called patriotic manners. We also pledge an allegiance oath. We do these things because we are proud of our country and the freedoms we have. These symbols remind us daily of our freedoms. Pity the people who have forgotten or make light of these freedoms. They are to be pitied!

First grader: "I plege elegas to the Fag of the Nine os Sac in a Amerrca and to the peppec for wic it sas one nasson onder God in the visebl wif libarte and jostis for all."

Maybe next time I should write about children's interpretation of the "Star-Spangled Banner"—"José, can you see?"

Bathroom Problems

At the tender ages of five to eight, children surely could not know about sex and boy-girl relationships. But unless you are extremely naive or blind, soon you discover that knowledge of sex is as complete at age five as at age fifty, experience being the difference.

However, there is a saving grace; bathrooms and attendant problems are acceptable, natural, and commonplace among the very young. There may be a long line-up of little ones waiting to use the single toilet and yet the door will stay open. It's not a matter of childish innocence, because we manage to teach that out of them. It's more a matter of the importance adults attach to sex and bodily functions. This appears to be an American social affair.

We have kindergartners who are completely "house-broken," while some third graders have to call home for clean clothes and mama to come help.

Some of the youngest know all the gutter talk and the filth jargon when we get them. Many sleep, eat, and live in one or two rooms in houses and apartments, so they experience life in its entirety.

Once I heard a commotion in the boys' outdoor bathroom. In I walked but saw no one. Then I noticed two pair of feet sticking out from underneath the stall. Two first graders were lying on the floor, one on top of the other, their pants down around their feet. I walked out, got a bucket of cold water and poured it on them over the top of the stall! While they were yelling, I slipped out. If they read this story, they will know it was I, and not some avenging angel, one time long ago, who poured water on their misdirected ardor!

***

A first grader related to his teacher that Bobby was showing "it" to everybody in the rest room. He then told her, "Don't worry. I've seen a million of 'em and that one wasn't a bit pretty!"

***

One kindergarten teacher kept hearing her timing bell ringing in the closed bathroom. She discovered the girls were timing each other to see how long it took them to "go."

***

Another kindergarten teacher noticed her bathroom was extra wet, especially one wall. After questioning the boys, she discovered they were having a contest to see who could "go" the highest!

***

One group was discussing the first sound heard each morning. A little girl told her group, "My daddy gets out of bed and 'poots' real loud!"

***

He was asked if he had any childhood diseases when very young. "Yes—diarrhea!"

***

Joe went to the bathroom and came back immediately with the idea that something was stopped up and wouldn't work. His buddy told him he knew how it was because his nose got stopped up and wouldn't work sometimes!

***

Gaston finally had his new glasses—a real victory for all of us! So the teacher happily asked the class what was different about Gaston. Johnny, a sharp little detective, correctly noted, "He's wet his britches!"
Gaston, not to be outdone, said, "It wasn't me!"

***

Note to the teacher: "Dere teacher, if roger hast to go to the bathroom let him go for i had to give him some mattson to take."

***

"Do you know where my teacher's office is?"
"No, where?"
"In the bathroom. That's where she takes you to paddle you!"

***

"please excuse Rene to go to the rest room. please it is real possible."

***

Rhonda ran up to her teacher on the playground and told her Harry was "hunching" all the girls behind the wall. Warren came running up and said, "That's okay. He's been hunching all the boys too!"

***

And from the boy's bathroom the tattler reported, "Ken was showing everything he had!"

***

While taking P.E. outside, Anita told the instructor she had to go to her room to use the bathroom. He told her to use the outside one. So she did! He turned around, and there she was, squatting in the middle of the field!

***

One: "My feet are getting wet!"
Two: "Yes, I know. I'm wetting my pants!"

***

They were washing hands to go to lunch. Jeff was at the doorway of the girls' rest room handing out towels. He gave each girl a towel while trying to keep his eyes covered so he would not see them coming out of their bathroom.

***

The commode was stopped up in one room, and the teacher was becoming frantic. Don told her, very calmly, "Don't worry, teacher. God promised us there'd be no more floods."

***

David was crying and trying to explain why he wet his pants: "Damn zipper wouldn't work!"

***

Comment on wetting pants: "He's a baby. I can hold it for four hours!"

***

The teacher explained about the many hardships the Pilgrims endured—no soap, no water, no privacy, and no bathrooms. Then she asked, "What do you suppose was the first thing they did when they landed?"

The answer, without hesitation: "Peed!"

***

The teacher brought Tommy into my office from the outside rest room. She hesitated, stammered, and stuttered. Finally I asked her what was wrong. She turned red, said the child would tell me and rushed from the office. Tommy had used the bathroom and then caught himself in his zipper. This was no little problem! Finally he was free, but I think the teacher suffered more than Tommy!

***

"Jane can't come to school today. She has loose vowels."

***

Mr. Hawkins, our truant officer, was asked to check at one house where they all hated him. He didn't like to go to their house. But, he went and was standing on the front porch talking to the mother when the three-year-old walked up and wet Hawkins's leg. They really all hated him!

***

Urgent message to the office: "The teacher said to hurry down to our room. The commode just flew over!" (I wonder if it was in formation?)

***

"My mother is going to have bladder surgery through her teeth."

* * *

"Teacher, I'm in a big hurry—I have to do number ten!"

* * *

Annie came into the office wet and wanted dry clothes. She told the secretary she had been afraid to ask to "go." The secretary explained the next time she got the "urge," just to go. Annie said she would. As she left the office, she turned and asked, "Say, what's the 'urge'?"

* * *

Girl entering the office: "Do you mind if I vomit in your bathroom?"

* * *

"How do you spell bathroom?"
"B-A-T-H-R-O-O-M. "
"Well, how do you spell foom?"
"What?"
"Foom! You know, like bathfoom!"

* * *

Chris was acting up. He would do nothing right. The teacher told him to go into the bathroom and straighten himself out. She heard him through the partition talking to himself, "Now, Chris, you gotta get yourself all straightened out—today! What are you gonna do about it? Okay, now get out there and get to work!"

* * *

"I hate my sister! She passes gas."

* * *

"My girl sits ugly in front of boys."

"How old is she?"

"Six."

***

"John is over there showing a magazine full of naked women!"

"Okay, Susie, I'll attend to it."

"Well, you'd better hurry! One of those women didn't have any clothes on!"

When You're Finished, Quit

The most difficult thing to do with this type of manuscript is to stop. There is always one more "funniest thing that ever happened" to add to your efforts. And as soon as it was announced my book was finished, people immediately wanted to know if I had included "such and such" or "so and so."

Even during the interview with Kathy, the kind newslady, a small girl wandered in my office wanting me to sew up her pants which had split. Kathy said this kind of proved what I had been saying about small children. However, as each day goes by, the unceasing flow of innocent humor continues.

Money and small children cause a lot of confusion and controversy, usually because they do not know the true relative value of each denomination:

George had four coins—two nickels and two quarters. Carolyn, the secretary, tried to show him how they were different. She touched one of the quarters eagle-side up, and asked, "What is this?"

He looked very closely, squinting, and then stated very solemnly, "That's a bird."

Asked why he had traded off his two pennies for another boy's quarter, Jon wisely related, "I know a real dumb kid who'll give me four pennies for this one!"

Charlie had been pestering me as I entered the building each day. He always had a dime or quarter for me to change into nickels or pennies. This day, however, he greeted me with a twenty and a ten—dollar bills, that is! I asked him where he got all that money. He said he had saved it and now wanted some pennies and other change. I told him to let his teacher keep the money for him. Then I tried to get his mother on the phone. Finally she was to have a message relayed to her that the school needed her, but there was no emergency.

About an hour later she rushed into my office wanting to know what the emergency was. I had to go over the entire story ending with the thirty dollars he wanted in change. Her mouth dropped open and she shouted out, "Thir-ty Dam-n Dol-lars! Where in hell did he get that kind of money? I don't even have two dollars of my own! Thir-ty Dam-n Dol-lars!"

***

Sometimes praise is wasted on them: "Joe, you did an excellent job of counting!"

"'Course I did. Ain't coming to school for nothing!"

***

Jackie confided to me, "Mr. Wilkins, I know what your wife's name is!"

So I asked, "What?"

He proudly announced, "Mrs. Wilkins!"

***

He told the teacher he couldn't write on that green-lined paper because it made his teeth hurt.

***

Todd said his father had to go to Yugoslavia for General Electric because G.E. had prostate trouble! (I never could figure that one out. Neither could his folks!)

***

And they'll tell on you! Donnie, a kindergartner had several dollars. When asked where the money came from, he stated, "Me and mama babysat."

Q: "Why do you have so much of it?"

A: "'Cause I did the babysitting."

Q: "What'd mama do?"

A: She stayed in bed with her boyfriend. You know, I'm not gonna do that when I grow up. It's not nice!"

***

A kindergartner told me, "My daddy died before I was born."

Me: "I'm sorry."

Her: "Yeah, in fact he died even before my mama and my daddy were married."

***

She was standing there waiting with the armload of beautiful flowers for her teacher. One of the other teachers stopped and commented, "Those are certainly pretty! Are they gladiolus?"

She quickly defended her flowers: "No, they're not Gladys Ole's! They're mine!"

***

I knew her nickname was "Boo," but for some strange reason I could not remember her real name. So I asked her what her first name was. She replied, "My first name is Boo. My last name is Sophia Jane Allison."

***

John was good so the aide gave him a ruler as a prize, saying, "John, this is a learning tool." About a week later the teacher threatened him with a ruler. He exclaimed, "No! No! You can't do that; a ruler is a learning tool!"

***

At lunch came a description of the cheese biscuits: "Those biscuits have chicken pox!"

***

She was looking for her mother: "Have you seen a woman with dark hair and polka dots?"

***

Did you know milk comes from marshmallows?

***

A third-grade student asked the librarian for a book on the Vikings. She looked through the number section for the Scandinavian stories—all about the Norseman and Eric the Red. She then asked him which particular Viking. He replied, "Carl Eller."

***

It was time for our school's "Country Fair." Robert had been pressured into service by his mother to carry in the tray of cupcakes. It was quite evident from the smears of chocolate all over his face he had eaten one of them on the way in. Before any questions were asked, he volunteered, "One of 'em fell off!"

***

Q: "What's that perfume your teacher has on today?"
A: "It's musk. Or did she say 'Jog'?"

***

David caught a squirrel and was holding it tightly behind its neck. His teacher asked him how he caught it without getting bitten, and to throw it down because it may have rabies. He said, matter of factly, "It did try to bite me, so I spanked it! And it doesn't have rabies because I looked it over real good."

***

Kindergartner: "I don't want to be a father, I want to be a motorcycle rider."

Helper: "Well, you could be a motorcycle rider in the daytime and a father at night!"

***

She came into the office, head bowed down, and mumbled something. I asked her what she had wanted and again came a soft mumble. Finally I had to get down in her face and said for her to tell me once more. This time I had no trouble understanding as she blurted out in no uncertain spitting terms, "I have the FLU!"

***

The music teacher saw Jimmy outside his room evidently banished from the classroom. She stopped to see what was wrong. He responded by asking her how to spell a real bad word—a real bad word which music teachers don't know how to spell! She was appalled and told Jimmy to go in and discuss it with his teacher. Later when she returned, there was Jimmy back out in the hallway. As she passed, he looked up and said, "Music Teacher, my teacher couldn't spell it either!"

***

There are many ways to let children know you like them. However, they will know how you feel in spite of what you do, especially if you can't stand the little heathens. You need eighteen hugs a day to stay healthy. I could always count on mine at school.

If you tell a child she is pretty, she will be pretty. If you tell a boy he can jump rope well, he will jump his head off. You should also smile, laugh, be patient, and gentle. Make them happy, be fair, and they will do better. Even if this wouldn't work, it'll make the teacher or parent feel better.

Over twenty studies have been made in the last twenty years concerning the "Rosenthal Effect." Robert Rosenthal's efforts have never been disproved by any of these studies. In essence, his work stated very simply says: "Smile, like children a lot, and the returns will be very fulfilling."

"Susan felt pretty yesterday, so I kept her home." So let's all try to feel pretty. It makes life so much more fun!

And so it continues—never really over. Some of it is beautifully original; some you've heard before in a different light. But to hear it and listen to it makes your life bearable when it's at its worst!

I know it has made life for me a real picnic! By the way, did I include the one about the school picnic? Oh, well . . .

About the Author

George Wilkins was born in Hendersonville, North Carolina, the youngest of nine children. The family lived in many states, from Virginia to California. He earned degrees in education and mathematics from North Carolina State University, the University of Tennessee, and Western Carolina University. He served in World War II for three years, then was recalled for duty in the Korean War for an additional three years.

George and his wife Cecile "Teal" Few Wilkins are the parents of five children, all married, and grandparents of twelve. The Wilkinses presently live in the Laurel Park area of Hendersonville.

Mr. Wilkins served as eighth grade teacher for two years at Hendersonville High School where he also was the assistant principal. Beginning in 1960, George served thirty-one years as principal of Bruce Drysdale Elementary School. Now retired, he plays in the Hendersonville Community Band, is a charter member of the Hendersonville Symphony, and writes a monthly column for the *Hendersonville Times-News*.